One in a Million

Coping with a Rare Cancer and Finding Strength You Didn't Know You Had

Paul Evans

Dedicated to my Mom - my inspiration and my rock.
Love you loads x

Contents

Introduction   1

February 2024 - Appendicitis eh?   3

Life Before Cancer   11

My "Urgent" CT scan   21

Meeting Mr Shariff   25
    °   HAMN (High-Grade Appendiceal
        Mucinous Neoplasm)
    °   Cytoreductive Surgery
    °   HIPEC

Bowel Prep – SOFT Toilet Wipes at The   33
Ready!

TikTok, You Don't Stop   39

Clearing Out   43

Birthday Celebrations   47

One Week To Go   51

The Day Before Surgery   57

21st May 2024 - The Big Day   61

EPOC (Enhanced Post Operative Care)   67

Let's Get Physical, Physical!   69

Recovery on The Ward   75

Seeing The Scar for The First Time   77

Time To Go Home   87

Home at Last   91

The Cancer Free Call   97

Life's an Adventure (poem)   101

Photos   102

Time For a Brew (poem)   107

Professor Beggs: the Man, the Myth, the Legend   109

Lynch Syndrome   111

Serrated Polyposis Syndrome   115

Let's Talk About the Diving Board   119

Fatigue: Batteries Not Included   121

Interpersonal Psychotherapy (IPP): Yikes That Sounds Scary!   125

Drawing My Way Back   129

These Boots Are Made For Walking   133

Dressed to De-Stress: Dopamine Dressing   137

Trauma and Cancer: More Than Just the   143
Physical Battle

Birds, birds, birds!   147

Feeding Yourself Back to Strength   153

Survivor's Guilt   157

Strength in Number: Cancer as a Community   161
and Support Network

Knee Op: Yes, ANOTHER Operation   165

Discovering My Identity   169

Top Tips   177

This Isn't the End, This Is Just the Beginning   179

Special Thanks   183

Introduction

8:30am - Monday, 18th March 2024
The day my life changed forever

I had been sitting on that hard hospital chair for over ten hours - tired, in pain and completely exhausted. I had little to no rest. What was going on?

The consultant doing his rounds came and pulled the curtain around my little chair area and sat down.

"You have this rare type of cancer that I've only read about and never actually seen. We'll need to get you an urgent CT scan and then arrange for you to see a specialist".

Hold on.
Cancer.
Did I hear him right?
Did he really say cancer?!

"Yeah, cancer. Cancer is a little like a car crash. Some are 80 to 90mph, yours is more like 30 to 40."

He said it so nonchalantly, it almost felt like he was telling me I'd only stubbed my toe. Then he stood up and left. I was alone. No "Are you ok? Is there anyone you need to speak to or stay here with you? Do you need a drink?" None of his team stayed, no nurses. No care, no empathy, no kindness. Just silence. I felt so alone. Was this real? Was this actually happening?

The first thought I had wasn't about me or my health at all. It was about my Mom. Is she gonna be ok? How can

I tell her this? Did I call her? Did I text her? I honestly can't remember. It's all a blur.

I had to stay in hospital overnight, so I needed stuff from home, but all I really needed was my Mom. I still feel sick reliving this moment; the way he told me was disgusting. Cold, clinical words that left me feeling utterly alone, confused and angry. To diagnose someone with a rare form of cancer in that manner is an utter disgrace. I don't wish that experience on anyone. However, this isn't where this journey started. That was a month before, with my appendix.

February 2024
Appendicitis eh?

Monday

I felt a twinge in my right side, just below my ribs. It was painful to touch and hurt loads, I knew something wasn't right. After the whole day deliberating, I decided to go to A&E at about 10:30pm.

A doctor examined me and concluded it was most likely IBS (irritable bowel syndrome), so go home and have some lansoprazole, that should sort it. I wasn't bloated or indigested. Something didn't feel quite right to me, surely this can't be IBS? The pain was sharp and to the side, like something was poking me. You know your own body and to me, it felt like something a little more serious.

Friday

The pain had increased significantly and become unbearable. I hadn't slept a wink, and I struggled to get out of bed. It felt like someone had their fingers under my rib cage, pulling it apart whilst a football had been inflated inside me. I was sweating from the agonising pain and knew I had to get up and go to hospital.

It took a while, every breath hurt, every movement had to be slow and steady. I managed to get dressed and order a taxi to A&E. I arrived about 9:30am. Utter chaos. The hospital was absolutely rammed. It was loud, bright, messy, it almost didn't feel real, like some sort of dystopian future. This billion-pound super hospital was only a few years old, what had happened?

People were slumped in chairs, talking loudly on their phones, chewing, crisp packets and empty coffee cups were strewn on the floor. It was disgusting. I felt like I was in a scene from The Walking Dead.

The hours passed. I sat in pain, in silence, respectful. Others, not so; shouting and moaning about how long they'd been waiting: I'd been there longer. I was near the vending machine, and the low hum and luminous lighting was giving me a headache. Come on man, you've got this! I waited for my turn. And boy, did I wait.

More hours passed. I didn't want to be there, but I wanted answers, I was desperate for help. Eventually, they called my name, and I was taken for a chest x-ray (I still have no idea why), and then a blood test.

Yet more hours went by. I still had no idea what was going on, no updates were given and I felt no sense of care. I was moved to another waiting area. I didn't ask why, I was so tired and the pain was increasing; I just followed the instructions.

Time wasn't a thing anymore. I'd been there about 7-8 hours, but it felt like a lifetime. This was taking its toll mentally, why wasn't someone taking this seriously? Why wasn't someone taking *me* seriously? I was determined to see a doctor and get some answers.

My name got called, this time by the surgical team. I went into the examination room, curtain pulled around me. Three doctors asked me what symptoms I had, how long they'd been there, if there was anything that had happened to cause this. I explained the extreme pain, pointed to the area and laid down on the bed to be examined. One of them prodded the area. "Ouch!! Yes, right there, just below my ribs".

The three of them got into a huddle, talking quietly and looking at me every now and then over their shoulders. What was so secretive? What were they talking about? Paranoia was kicking in. After a brief discussion, they decided that it was another team that needed to examine me further, a chest expert.

I was then back out of the examination room. No seats were left in the waiting area, so I stood in the corridor leaning against the cold, slippy wall. I tried to look as composed as I could. Others were doing the same, I couldn't believe how busy it was.

A chest consultant came and found me.

"Paul?"

He immediately put his finger on my ribs right where my pain was and I flinched. He'd sought me out because he knew I was being "fobbed off" by the surgical team.

"If I hadn't come down here to see you, you would've waited for hours on end, it's clearly not your chest".

I felt relieved…Someone who cared. Someone who saw me as a patient, not a nuisance. But now I was back in what felt like an endless loop of waiting for the surgical team again. I felt angry, exhausted, hungry and alone.

It gets a little blurry now but I believe I was then moved to yet another area, slightly quieter but still very busy. I took a seat. It was now after 11pm, 14 hours of being in hospital, waiting, without any information or clarity. I wanted to go home; I hadn't eaten all day.

I found a nurse. She informed me that if I left now, the process would have to start all over again tomorrow, the waiting, the examining. So, to have a seat for the night. A seat, not a bed.

I started hyper fixating on noise. The person in front of me had been speaking to her boyfriend on loudspeaker for hours. By 1am I'd had enough: "Come on, this is a hospital, the lights are off, I'm trying to sleep".

That was my very English stiff upper lip kicking in, rather than the Brummie in me that probably would've just yelled "shut it!!". Seriously, why are people so selfish nowadays? The lack of thought for others astounds me.

The waiting felt tortuous; I couldn't rest, I was in pain and my anxiety levels were continually increasing. I knew I had to get through this and luckily, I can be stubborn when I need to be! Something wasn't right and if I had to wait, then dammit, I just had to wait.

The morning came and eventually I had a scan, an ultrasound. It was painful as they pressed the probe onto me, but the team were very caring. The technician said they couldn't see anything on the screen as it was "cloudy", so a CT (computed tomography) scan would be needed.

I waited…and waited…and waited. I had been in hospital for 32 hours now, mostly sat on a horribly hard and uncomfortable chair. I didn't know if I was still in A&E, nor did I know what was happening. It really felt like I had been put somewhere and forgotten about. Almost like that tin of soup that went out of date in 2008 that you find when clearing out your cupboards. Oh, I forgot about you, hiding there in the back!

I finally got the CT scan. The technician noted something didn't look right; she said it looked like blood or mucus was coming out of my appendix, but that a consultant would need to look it over to determine the results. This didn't sound good at all.

My Mom came to visit me, oh how I needed my Mom! She immediately brought a smile to my face, just don't hug me too hard ha! Thankfully, I had been transferred onto a trolley at this stage, there were still no beds available. Time passed and it was amazing to have my Mom there for support. I even joked, "Hope it's not my appendix".

The consultant came in to discuss my CT scan results. *"Appendicitis, eh? Who would've thought?"*

The irony…. Google, that's who. Now, we should never trust Dr Google for anything as it always gives us the worst-case scenario, but in this case, my symptoms were classic appendicitis. It ticked all the boxes. The non caring arrogance in his voice still aggravates me. I imagined karate kicking his head, but alas, that was just my imagination.

Mt thoughts took over; Why wasn't I given the CT scan earlier? Surely that would have cleared this all up a lot sooner I wouldn't have had the torture of waiting so long with a lack of any sleep or rest.

I knew appendicitis was serious. I had heard that if your appendix bursts it can be fatal, so I anticipated immediate action, emergency surgery to remove it.
"Can't today, it's too late now for surgery". Said so very casually.

Fine, nil by mouth continues and the procedure will be tomorrow. I didn't sleep much as I continued to wait patiently.

I waited and waited. 7:30pm came and I said to a nurse "I guess no surgery then?"
"No, there was an emergency."

Fair enough, I can appreciate things like that happen, it is a hospital after all. Nil by mouth again until tomorrow. It would have been nice to be updated though I thought to myself. I was in a daze, neither asleep nor awake. Was this my life now? Stuck on loop, Groundhog Day.

Tomorrow came, another emergency, so no surgery again. I'm not sure how I got through any of this. Sleep deprivation, no food and minimal water, no updates until I pressed for them. My fight kicked in, my determination, my need to survive. It was almost like none of it was real, an out of body experience, viewing myself sat on that chair from a far.

Five days after I was admitted, I finally had the appendectomy. I don't really remember much apart from the morning; around 7am someone came and said something like:

"Right, we are taking you down next, you're first on the list for surgery today".

I so remember thought that I felt relief. I'm sure I had to sign consent forms and I'm sure I was spoken to by the surgical team, the anaesthetists, the nurses, assistants etc, but I have no recollection.

I was put to sleep. The keyhole surgery lasted about an hour and a half and after recovery, I was moved to my own room; at last, something decent! Not exactly 5 stars, but it'll do!

The surgeon came by to let me know how everything had gone and that my appendix had *"obliterated"* inside me. I felt anger. My appendix had not only burst but burst to the extreme that he used the word "obliterated". Again, my mind went back to questioning why the surgery wasn't done sooner. Why wasn't I treated? Why didn't I matter?

I needed rest, I need antibiotics and I needed to stay overnight for observation. Most of all, I needed a brew! Oh, how fantastic that first cuppa was. Three cups of tea in an hour and some bourbon biscuits; I could get used to this! The nurses found it funny and they definitely made me feel looked after.

Two days later, blood drained removed and patched up, I went home. I was advised to go back to hospital if I felt any pain in case an abscess had formed. Biopsies had been taken for testing during surgery. It all sounded pretty standard to me, let's get back to normality.

At home, I rested. I was bruised and knew I'd have some scars, but I had a story to tell. I was tired and in pain but give it a few weeks and I'd be back in the gym. That's right, Love Island bod here I come!

Now for a huge realisation. For the first time in my life, I realised I wanted to LIVE, I wanted to survive. Depression had been a constant in my life. The truth of it all? I hated my life. I hated being single. I hated being stuck in a freelance role where I felt underappreciated and taken for granted. I hated feeling like a failure in every aspect of my life.

However, the reality of how fragile life actually is had hit me hard. I didn't want this to be the end. I wanted to make plans, to see friends, to have holidays and to travel. I wanted to find love again. I wanted to live and enjoy life.

But it turns out that life had other plans. BIG ol' plans. One month later, that original twinge was back, albeit slightly different, and I returned to A&E as I had been advised. I got seen a lot faster this time round. That's more like it, positive vibes.

An A&E doctor informed me that my biopsies happened to be back and *"not to worry, definitely not cancer"* but to stick around so that one of the consultants could see me. Phew! NOT CANCER! Maybe it was just abscess. *"Take a seat over there"*. Fine, I can handle that; More waiting but I've been here before, I can wait.

At 2:30am a member of the surgical team came to see me. She said that the consultant would write to me, or I could stay until the morning so that he could discuss the biopsy results. I mean, why would I leave at this point?! Sit back, try to get some sleep.

Then 8:30am came and that's when my life changed forever.

Life Before Cancer

Wow, writing this makes me realise that it's actually hard for me to envision that there *was* a life before all this. But there was…....

1982 - A volley of thunder, a blitz of lightning and a crash of rain hit the hospital window…oh, hold on, I've gone back way too far! Let's get back on track.

2023 - Before this all kicked off, I was a depressed, anxious, bearded and bald Brummie – and yet somehow still single with all that going for me! I really was just plodding through life the best I could. My Mom was my constant, she's understanding, kind, caring; she always champions me and she is my inspiration. A hug from my Mom has always helped ground me.

We spend every Christmas together and every Birthday. We had been through so much together, but little did we know that there was so much more to go through just around the corner.

My best mate Millsy is literally the best bloke I've ever met, kind, humble, hilarious and just sound! He would do anything for anyone and does! We've known each other since we were 11 when I destroyed him in a table tennis match at school (I still like to remind him now and then). Then we lived together at Uni with another legend, the Big Man. We all have the same sense of humour, very David Brent. A silly text from Millsy would always cheer me up, even on my darkest days. What a geezer. For years we've met up EVERY Tuesday for a PlayStation night and now and then, when we can, we visit the Big Man. True friendship that lasts.

My Home

I live alone in a house that was built in 1906. As soon as I walked through the door, I knew it was for me, it had the right energy, the right look and it was just what I'd been searching for.

Now, it's not perfect by any stretch, it's absolutely freezing in the winter and boiling in summer. My first winter there, the 20-year-old boiler packed up and I ended up wearing two fleeces, a woolly hat, and a scarf INSIDE. The windows don't keep out the noise and it'll creek and make odd noises all the night; it's not haunted, it's just old…I hope!

Maybe the house was a reflection of myself? Quirky, a bit battered, but full of life and character. It has amazing high ceilings - even higher for me as I'm only 5'5"!

I've made it a home with all my little quirks – art on the walls, funky cushions, rugs, skull ornaments, too many tea mugs to count, a dark green kitchen, a dark blue bedroom, it all suits its style and age. There are lots of plants that just about survive (that reminds me, I must water them)! I have a 1970's drink cabinet shaped like a globe, a terrarium, an Audrey 2 toy from Little Shop of Horrors on display, and just general bits and bobs on show! I love all my knick-knacks and kooky items. It's mine and I love it! It's my safe place and I feel comfy here. It's opposite the canals which means I can have an amazing walk whenever I want. I have one really nice set of neighbours who put up my reindeer horn ceiling light (not real of course). The other neighbours, well, that could be a whole other book, and they don't deserve any more time than that.

Health

I've briefly mentioned depression and anxiety, but I also have asthma which is well controlled, and I've had stomach issues for a few years.

One of the worst experiences of my life was having an endoscopy. There was a potential that I had pancreatic cancer, so an endoscopy was scheduled. I cannot tell you how hard and horrible this was. My body just shut down, my eyes were streaming, I was gagging and felt like I was choking. I'm not sure if it's because I have asthma, but I couldn't breathe, I grabbed the wire of the camera, a big NO NO. They stopped. I sat up in silence.

They said I'd need to schedule another one and to be put to sleep next time. But how long would this take? I was worried that I was seriously ill. I was there, my stubbornness and determination kicked in: "Can we try one last time?"

"Of course". Phew. I laid on my side, the nurse held my hand, they sprayed my throat, lubed up the camera and slowly slid it down my oesophagus. Every 5-10 seconds my reflux kicked in, I was gagging, choking, crying - this was horrible. The nurse continued to hold my hand, letting me know she was there and that I was doing well. It only lasted 5 minutes but felt like torture, but I got through it.

Sleep has always been an issue for me and since the age of 11 I've really struggled with insomnia. I find it hard to settle, to turn off my mind. Once I do drift off, the sleep is broken, almost in limbo between awake and asleep. I wake up every hour or two and when I wake up, I WAKE

UP, fully aware. Then, back to the process of trying to sleep, trying to settle, trying to stop overthinking. it's a vicious cycle.

It's affected every part of my life and sometimes who and how I am. My temperament changes. The way I feel about myself and others changes. My motivation to do anything is affected. Food, drink, gym, friends, family, relationships have all suffered.

I vividly remember my alarm being set for 7am for work and checking the clock, counting down how many hours sleep I had left, 5,4,3,2 hours…oh man, it's been so tough throughout the years. Unless you've had broken sleep for this long, it's really hard to explain. I see other people who have less sleep than they're used to and they're different to their usual selves. Well, I know how different I can be; in a daze, a zombie just walking through life and trying to survive off a few hours rest. Rest that others take for granted.

Work Life and Frustrations

After getting a 2:2 (also known as a drinker's degree) in Film and TV from Aberystwyth University, I set my sights and hopes high - first the BBC, then Hollywood! I was so proud of getting a degree and absolutely loved my time at Uni.

The BBC and Hollywood? Well, that didn't quite work out but shopping TV sounds glamorous though, right? Believe me, it wasn't. At times it felt like juggling flaming torches whilst riding a unicycle - naked. The magic had gone. The hope had gone. It was beaten out of me by a toxic work environment, arrogant and bullying managers, producers thinking they were the best thing ever, ordering the floor staff to do this and do that. Maybe I didn't exactly take their point of view. Maybe my objection to being treated like that ruffled a few feathers, but hey ho, I'm not being treated like dirt.

I did however meet some truly wonderful people who became friends and who made it worthwhile. I'm still in touch with a lot of the good ones, Irish Matt, Will, Ollie, Steve, Eric, Guy, Adelaide, Chris P, Hannah and John to name a few. Genuine, kind and amazing people with positive energy.

Some days I loved, some days I dreaded but most of the time it felt like being stuck in a toxic soap opera with terrible scripts. You give it your all, but somehow, your passion gets mistaken for weakness or *"too much enthusiasm."* One day you're the go-to expert, the next you're a ghost.

The job just about paid the bills, but my dreams? Those packed their bags and left without me. It took me years to realise that it was JUST a job, and I simply needed it to pay my mortgage. I still gave it my all, I was creative and passionate until the end. My sarcasm and humour got me through the toughest days; I really didn't care if no one got the jokes, the worse the pun, the better!

I was a floor manager, camera operator, director and then producer. I used my own way of doing things, being enthusiastic, talking through what was happening, actually doing my job well! For some reason, this rubbed certain people up the wrong way. The good ones loved me and that's all that mattered in the end, I was genuine.

Being a freelancer was tough, I had to mask myself and work with 12 different teams, different shifts, different times, different expectations, different targets, and different frustrations. I was the only person that had ever worked for all 5 separate channels, all with their own way of doing things.

As the producer, the expectation was that I would be an expert on all these subjects, products and sales. I was head of the team, if the sales failed, it was me would bear that. It was draining to mask who I was. If my shifts were cancelled, I simply had to take it and smile, more would hopefully come up. I had to "play the game", something which I despised.

Christmas and New Year were particularly hard as everyone wants it off, so you're the first person asked. You do what's needed to get by and pay your bills but it was hard and I don't think I was ever thanked or praised. I was a commodity.

On the flip side, I still made light of situations, most likely by saying "that's what she said" at least ten times a day to get me through!

My favourite job role was "Channel Planner" for Lifestyle TV. My manager Guy made the role specifically for me; what a bloke! This actually gave me freedom and made me feel worthwhile. I could use my methodical approach and combine it with creativity to plan shows and programming. We were a fantastic team with tons of ideas and hopes. We wanted to make it the best channel there was, make it interesting, engaging, fun and at the end of the day, smash our targets.

Alas, due to wider business reasons, the channel shut down. It was such a shame. Office politics played its part, favouritism played its part. It was the smallest channel and needed cutting. I was gutted, to return to uncertainty. Back to not knowing what shifts I'd have and to constantly

fighting and grabbing anything I could "that's what she…"
(Oh, never mind).

Tattoos

The year before my cancer diagnosis was an especially tough one for me. My depression was at an all-time high. The way I'd describe it is falling into a mud pit, trying to claw your way out, with the mud seeping under your nails, your trainers constantly slipping and you slipping further and further down into the darkness. I was really struggling.

My anxiety was constantly telling me that I wasn't good enough, that I couldn't achieve anything, and the 'what ifs and maybes' took over my daily thoughts. It had to stop, but how could it? I needed something to change. *I* needed to change.

One thing I'd always been interested in was tattoos. My style and clothes changed all the time; what if one day I want tons of tatts and the next day I don't? What if I wear a smart suit and the tattoos don't go with it? What if, what it, what if?

I was 41; if not now, then never! I researched LOADS and decided I wanted traditional patch work tattoos, Sailor Jerry style. I met a wonderful artist, Ally, who helped me so much. She was a tattoo artist and a therapist rolled into one!

In about two and a half months I'd gone from zero to 23 tatts!! The other artists called me crazy but respected how I'd had so many in such little time. Both arms were covered, my elbow (ouch) my chest (double ouch) and my sternum (the only one I had to stop halfway because of the pain!). They range from things that mean stuff to me - of course I have a cup of tea "storm in a teacup" on my arm

- to some that reflect my silly personality: "that's what she said" but in Latin. My favourite films are represented, Silence of the Lambs with a death head moth, Casablanca with a gin bottle, skull and crossbones for The Goonies, vampire lips for Lost Boys and a quote from A Clockwork Orange.

They say tattoos become an obsession, which I can kinda see as they can reflect different parts of your personality, but man they hurt!! Don't let anyone say they don't! Later on, I'll discuss the ones I had a few months after my operation.

Hopes and Dreams

What did I want out of life? Honestly, I wasn't sure anymore. I honestly didn't think I'd make it to 40. I don't say that lightly - depression was and is a horrible disease. I'd only ever been in love once. Back then I imagined having a family, holidays, an amazing home etc, that was the dream, right? That was "normal".

Maybe I just wanted some sort of stability, I certainly couldn't get that as a freelancer. A little happiness - not much to ask for right? Not to feel invisible, to feel seen and heard. Deep down I hoped for more than just "getting by" but I'd stopped daring to dream big. I always felt like I failed.

I've always fantasised about how life could or should be, usually the simple things, the nice things. I have huge empathy and want others to do well, but I also wanted that for myself. Life needed to change and boy, was it gonna!

Walking - oh how this helped give me so much peace and keep me calm. During lockdown I was walking 35 miles a week until an old football knee injury came back.

Now, I wasn't exactly a great footballer, far from it, but tearing my meniscus HURT. It also turned out my ACL was torn, cue two knee ops!

Living a stone's throw from the canal system (Birmingham has more canals than Venice - FACT) meant that I got to connect with nature, to hear the trees rustle in the wind and to see a heron most days. This elegant bird that looked like it owned the place; Calm and graceful, a reminder that there's beauty even in the chaos. Nature truly is a healer. I was able to widen my perspective, to not be hindered by a phone screen, laptop, or tv screen, to look up at the wider world and sky. No headphones, let's listen to nature, let's see all the little ducks and avoid the notoriously angry Brummie geese! I had my backpack, stainless steel water bottle, hiking boots and was ready to go wherever I could. I have no sense of direction, so sometimes I'd get lost even a mile from home!

Music

From Black Sabbath to UB40 (fellow brummies!) my music taste has always been eclectic. At Uni, myself, Millsy and Big Man all bought the Blue album, our guilty pleasure and so much fun! If I put my music on shuffle today, it'll be a mix of classic 80's, Korn, Duran Duran, Elvis, The Beatles, Amy Winehouse, Tupac and then Dean Martin. I love having a varied taste in music, it's what life is all about!

Films and TV

As I did a degree in this subject, I guess you could say I enjoy them! My favourtie films include Casablanca, The Goonies, One Flew Over the Cuckoo's Nest, Goodfellas, The Lost Boys, Step Brothers, Parasite, American Pie, A

Clockwork Orange, The Shining, Silence of the Lambs, the list goes on and on! In lockdown I decided to write a top 10 favourites list and I wrote over 100 down ha!

The same can be said for TV, the list constantly grows; Sopranos, Breaking Bad, The Office (UK and American), Peep Show, Game of Thrones, Dexter and Alan Partridge to name a few! Good old Bargain Hunt is a daily watch, and I'd love to go on it!

Fashion

Then there's my fashion. Oh man how I love my clothes. I've always felt more confident in certain clothing; I love something a little different. The funkier the shirt the better, the more leopard print the better! I love my trainers, and I love a classic, retro vibe. I'm not scared to wear something daring, is that a T-rex breathing fire with lasers out of its eyes and Santa on its back for my Xmas jumper? You're damn right it is!! Clothes are still a huge part of me and I'll delve into "dopamine dressing" in a later chapter.

My "Urgent" CT Scan

Right, back to Cancer now. My CT scan was planned for 8:30am. I'd been allowed to go home the night before so had a lovely veg curry with my Mom. I can't remember much about this time, if we watched a film, if we spoke about the diagnosis and "what's next", or if we just decided to have a day off as it were. One thing I know, is that my Mom has and always will be there for me, no matter what.

The nurses told me that I'd need to be back at hospital for 6:30am as I was still technically admitted. I got back to the ward right on time and explained to the secretary on the desk that I was there for my scan, she seemed very angry with me:

"That's not how it works, you can't just turn up for one"

I told her "I know, it's booked, I've still got my hospital band on my wrist. I was told I could go home and come back. I was tired and had been in hospital for two days and then allowed to go home last night".

"Well, I don't think that's happening, you can't just go home and then just turn up and expect a CT…oh hold on, I can see a note here".

Why is everything so blooming tricky?! Finally, she confirmed that yes, I was scheduled for a CT scan. Which I already knew!

No beds, so I was back in the waiting room on those horrible chairs again. I remember the luminescent green walls, disgusting, not exactly calming or tranquil. 8:30am came and went. A porter turned up at 9:15am and my scan was done about 9:30am. You lie back; they pop in a cannula and then inject you with this purple dye. The weird thing about this dye? Oh, it makes you think you've wet yourself! You get a warm sensation down there, it's very odd! The scan didn't take too long which was a relief.

I was taken back upstairs. This was my urgent scan, it was done specifically so that a cancer specialist could look at it, no one else in the hospital. I said thanks and was about to leave.

"You can't just leave; a doctor needs to look at your scan".

The same angry person on the desk as before. I explained what it was, who it was for and why I was going to leave. Then, the self-doubt trickled in, what if someone here does know more and you leave? Maybe if I stay, they can explain better than the previous consultant. I've waited more than this before, I can wait again, it'll only be an hour, right?

Midday came and went, eventually a doctor came to see me and told me that he didn't know what he was looking at and that I'd need a specialist. I was too tired to feel anger; it wasn't his fault. I knew I had cancer and didn't want feelings of frustration to get on top of me.

Now I had to wait for a discharge letter. Before leaving I asked if there was anyone I could speak to. The lack of empathy was back, *"yeah, your cancer expert".* Great, thanks, time to go before I exploded from the rage I felt.

I left and went straight home. I was overwhelmed, tired, upset, angry, emotional, frustrated. It felt like I'd been hit with a machine gun of information. I couldn't take it, I needed rest. I messaged my Mom to say I was home and that I was going to bed.

The next day I got up early. I knew I had a lot to do; I called MacMillan. Wow, they are truly amazing! The care, advice, empathy and understanding from everyone I spoke to was such a relief. I felt respected and that I mattered.

They wanted to help me. I'd highly recommend anyone affected by cancer to call them, for a chat, for advice, for comfort.

I spoke to various people over nearly two hours. There was lots of information to take in. Different departments help with different thing, clinical advice, financial advice etc. I wrote down a ton of notes.

After the call, I simply curled up into a ball on the floor. I was struggling. There was so much information and I was overwhelmed. I knew I had things to deal with, my mortgage being the top of my list. It's crazy, I'd been told I had cancer, yet the top of my list was my mortgage, not my health or wellbeing. I'd written a list of who I'd need to contact. But that would have to wait until tomorrow, I was wiped out, so back to bed it was.

In bed, the 'why me?' crept in and all the 'what ifs' came back again. Was this the end of my story? The fragility of life really came into play. What do I need to do? I haven't got a will. How will my Mom cope? Did I want to be buried? How would my funeral look? Do I want people in black and sad, or shall I make it quirky and fun to celebrate, ask everyone to wear funky shirts, record a silly video message to play and have fun music? These things were whirring round my head, over and over. My emotions were heightened, yet I hadn't cried. It was weird, I was just numb.

It actually took a few months before any tears were shed. I'd had a nice bottle of red wine, maybe more than I should have, and felt emotional. It wasn't forced; it was natural. I didn't cry much, but it was a release at last.

How did I deal with things? Sometimes I don't know, I'm stubborn I guess, I wanted to live and survive. This couldn't be the end. My life hasn't been amazing; I've only been in love once; I haven't explored everywhere I wanted to explore; I hadn't done enough!

My Mom was also a huge factor. I couldn't let her down, I needed to, no, I *wanted* to survive for her.

For each appointment, I made the conscious decision that nothing happened until it happened - nothing is real until they tell me the facts. I was methodical and structured in my approach. I wanted this cancer gone; I'd take all the advice given to me and get any test they wanted. Trust them, they're experts. Trust the process.

Appointments came and went. They were marked on the calendar for me to see. This and only this were on the days where they were scheduled. I knew this was beginning to be an issue, my whole day was focussed on a one-hour appointment. I wouldn't do anything else, no plans, no leaving the house, nothing. I had to supersede the appointments, have something on top of them to look forward to.

Pizza, curry, ice cream, chocolate, a film, see my Mom, my mates - whatever it was, THAT would be my focal point of the day, not the appointment. It's an amazing shift in your mindset to do this. To say, yes, my appointment is 2pm, BUT I have PIZZA at 6pm! It didn't always work out, but it was an aim and that's the main thing. You can't always achieve your goals but you can give them a go.

Meeting Mr Shariff

Kindness, compassion, empathy. Real care and consideration. That's how I'd describe Mr Shariff; the person that did my surgery and saved my life.

April - one month after my initial diagnosis and my first and only face to face appointment with Mr Shariff. The hospital was an hour's drive away, so I picked my Mom up and we went together.

The journey was fine; we were both probably a little more quiet than usual. I'm sure I had some funky songs on the radio to lighten the mood.

The hospital looked…hmm, different. Let's say the design was almost 1960's sci-fi futuristic architecture, which did make me laugh. Another bad film set for me to imagine I was on. We sat down and waited to be called.

We didn't have to wait long, the specialist Mr Shariff was only there to see me (what a legend). We went into his office, and he introduced himself. Firstly, he apologised for how I'd been treated and diagnosed. He acknowledged this wasn't right but from now on, under his care, that would change. I trusted him. He introduced the colorectal nurse that was with him. He asked me to lie down so he could examine my stomach. "Please don't cut into and ruin my tattoo" I joked. Pointing at the death head moth on my sternum. Making light of a very dark situation helped to ground me. He smiled. I sat back down.

He went through the details of the type of cancer I had, how it was in the lining of my appendix, so no blood tests or markers would ever show it, that when my appendix burst, it had released cancerous cells inside me, but they were contained inside the peritoneal sac.

"You have a rare form of cancer called HAMN…your CT scan and biopsies show a mix of high-grade and low-grade cancer".

HAMN (High-Grade Appendiceal Mucinous Neoplasm)

That discussion with Mr Shariff was the first time I had heard the word HIGH GRADE. The world suddenly stopped. Everything stopped. Everything closed in around me. High grade? What does that mean? Am I going to die? I felt sick.

He could clearly see I was in shock and upset. He spoke slowly and carefully, asking if I needed him to stop for a moment. I was stunned, silent, I just wanted him to carry on and let me know the next step. The words 'high grade' still has an effect on me today. This was not some "simple" cancer, this was serious, dangerous. I always focus back on the day I was diagnosed, the nonchalant way of trying to compare it to a 30-40mph road crash as opposed to one at 80-90mph. Well, high grade didn't sound like that now, high grade sounded pretty bloody scary.

He explained in more details. Then, came the big part of the appointment, my options. When you get to this part of the conversation, you actually have a choice of treatments. You can refuse all if you like. You can even take your business elsewhere as it were.

Option Number 1- let's go as aggressive as possible. This was called cytoreductive surgery. He would open me up, remove as much cancerous cells as possible, remove 30% of my bowel, remove the lining of my peritoneal sac and then whilst in surgery I would have something called

26

HIPEC (Hyperthermic Intraperitoneal Chemotherapy), also known as a "chemo wash".

Option number 2…I stopped him, there was no option 2 for me, I'd already made up my mind before the meeting, I wanted this cancer gone and I wanted it gone as quickly as possible: "Option 1, let's go aggressive".

He was glad that I chose that; he said some people like time to think and reflect but also go away regretting not taking that option. Some people even opt for no operation at all.

I'd brought along a MacMillan guide, questions to ask, but I didn't look at it once. He was thorough and talked through pretty much everything I needed to know. I probably asked a few questions, but I can't remember now.

He was unable to do the operation in April. Wow I hadn't even thought it would be that quick! So, most likely it would be mid to late May. At least I wouldn't be in hospital for my birthday!

The appointment was over. There was a lot of information to think about. The collateral nurse gave me her direct line to call her if I needed anything or thought of any questions. My Mom and I walked back to the car park, I'm not sure much was said. I really wish I hadn't driven there. It was hard to digest all that I'd been told, I was upset, emotional, a little angry, my Mom kept me calm and as always, was there when I needed her. I just know I didn't enjoy the drive home. It felt hard, like more and more people were driving like idiots, just to annoy me, not indicating, going too slow, too fast, going OVER a roundabout. My frustrations were showing. I dropped my Mom back to hers and I went home.

Digesting the information took time. If my appendix was taken out before it had obliterated would this still mean that I'd have to have this majorly intrusive operation? Did the initial hospital mess this up royally? What if this, what if that? Surely them not doing the appendectomy earlier created a domino effect? The burst appendix released cancerous cells, meaning major surgery and complications. Was someone to blame or at fault? Was *I* to blame? Your mind plays tricks, especially with years of anxiety and depression, you ALWAYS blame yourself. I felt isolated, unsure, upset, and alone.

At a glance: HAMN

- A rare type of aggressive tumour that starts in the appendix and produces lots of mucus - think of it as a jelly-like substance. The appendix isn't just a useless organ; when tumours grow here, they can cause big problems.
- It is more common in people over 50 but can occur at any age.
- Diagnosis is often difficult and needs specialist care. Often diagnosis is made late because early symptoms are vague or absent.
- HAMN is high-grade, meaning the cells look more aggressive under the microscope and have a higher chance to spread and cause serious illness.
- It's not common - you're now part of a special club: **One in a Million.**
- Because it makes so much mucus, HAMN can lead to a condition called pseudomyxoma peritonei, where mucus fills the abdomen and causes

swelling, pain and other issues. I was glad this wasn't the case for me.

- Treatment usually involves surgery to remove the tumour and any mucus buildup. Often, HIPEC is used after surgery to mop up any leftover cancer cells. I'll explain more about HIPEC in the next chapter.

- Getting a diagnosis for HAMN can be tricky, and it often takes specialist teams with experience in rare cancers to manage it. It's a scary diagnosis, but with the right treatment, many patients have hope.

- **Symptoms:** Abdominal swelling, pain, digestive issues.

- **Outlook:** With proper treatment, many patients manage the disease, but monitoring is crucial.

Cytoreductive Surgery

Cytoreductive surgery (CRS) is a major operation aimed at removing as much visible cancer from the abdominal cavity as possible. The goal is simple but tough - physically cut away every tumour and cancerous deposit the surgeon can see or feel, so only microscopic disease is left behind.

It's often used for cancers that have spread within the peritoneum (the lining of the abdomen) rather than through the bloodstream to distant organs. In many cases, it's combined with HIPEC (heated chemotherapy) to target any cells too small to see during surgery.

This isn't a quick operation and can last anywhere from six to fourteen hours, depending on how much disease there is and how complex the removal becomes.

It's one of the most demanding procedures in cancer treatment, both for the surgical team and for the patient.

Surgeons may remove sections of affected organs, including parts of the bowel, spleen, gallbladder, or sections of the peritoneum itself. Every case is different - some people lose very little tissue; others require multiple organ resections to achieve the best possible result.

Because it's such a major operation, recovery can be slow and intense. It often means weeks in hospital, followed by months of building up strength and mobility at home. But for some patients, this combination of aggressive surgery and targeted chemo offers the best chance of long-term survival.

At a glance: Cytoreductive Surgery

- **Purpose:** To physically remove as much visible cancer as possible from the abdominal cavity.
- **Commonly used for:** Peritoneal surface cancers (e.g. appendiceal cancer, colorectal cancer with peritoneal spread, mesothelioma of the peritoneum).
- **Procedure time:** 6–14 hours depending on complexity.
- **May involve:** Removal of affected organs or sections of tissue (bowel, spleen, gallbladder, peritoneum).
- **Often paired with:** HIPEC to target microscopic cancer cells left behind.
- **Recovery:** Weeks in hospital, months at home. Full recovery can take a year or more.

HIPEC (Hyperthermic Intraperitoneal Chemotherapy)

Wow, that's a mouth full ("that's what she…"

Sorry!). HIPEC is an intense, targeted cancer treatment that happens after surgery. Doctors remove as much visible tumour as they can, then bathe the inside of your abdomen with heated chemo drugs — think of it as a deep clean for the areas cancer might be hiding.

The 40° heat helps the chemo work better, penetrating tissue more effectively and killing off tiny cancer cells that surgery might miss. It's used mainly for cancers that have spread inside the abdomen, like certain bowel, ovarian, or peritoneal cancers.

Not every hospital does HIPEC - it's specialised and only available in certain centres. The treatment isn't suitable for everyone, and doctors carefully assess each case to decide if it's the right path.

HIPEC isn't a walk in the park. It's a long, complex operation that can take several hours under general anaesthetic, followed by a tough recovery. But for some people, it offers the best chance to control or even beat the disease. It's a game changer for some patients, providing a fighting chance when other options are limited. But it's no magic bullet - the journey can be challenging, and support is vital.

At a glance: HIPEC

- A specialised treatment used during surgery to target cancer cells inside the abdominal cavity with the aim of improved local cancer control and sometimes extended survival.

- After visible tumours are removed, heated chemotherapy is circulated in the abdomen to kill any remaining microscopic cancer cells.

- The heat (41–43°C) boosts the effectiveness of the chemotherapy and helps it penetrate tissue matter better.

- The heated chemo is administered for about 60 to 90 minutes during the operation.

- Commonly used for cancers such as peritoneal mesothelioma, colorectal, ovarian, and rare abdominal cancers like HAMN.

- Always combined with cytoreductive surgery.

- It's a major procedure with significant recovery time and risks but can improve survival in select patients.

- Recovery can be tough and includes the risk of infection, bleeding, and organ stress.

- Only certain specialist centres offer HIPEC due to its complexity and it isn't suitable for everyone. Selection depends on cancer type, spread, and overall health.

Bowel Prep - SOFT Toilet Wipes at The Ready!

Toilet humour, farting and jokes about poo always make you laugh right? Well, unfortunately in bowel prep the fun side is pretty hard to find. Butt (ha!), here we go…

The idea for bowel prep is that you drink a formula, and it flushes your system ready for a colonoscopy. This is done so that when the camera enters your bowel, the technician has a much clearer view and is able to detect more polyps, especially serrated ones as they can hide. The team even give you a score on how clear your bowel is! Now, I have a competitive edge, so I wanted a decent blooming score!

'You just drink the prep' - Sounds easy right? WRONG! The formula for bowel prep is RANK. Imagine drinking a pint of salt that has a chemically tropical fruit flavour, slightly gloopy, and you're halfway there to understanding.

I've had to have 4 lots of prep within 8 months: Colonoscopy, complex polypectomy, my cancer surgery and finally another complex polypectomy. You'll have your one meal of the day before 9am - breakfast will be a high carb meal as you're on a strict diet. I opted for crumpets, probably 4 as I knew I wouldn't be eating for about 28 hours. You have two packets of prep, one for day one, usually around 6pm, and one for the next day, usually 6am (I'd highly recommend 4:30am if your scan is 10am, DO NOT RISK IT!).

The packets are labelled and contain slightly different ingredients. You open packet one, mix the sachets into a jug of water, stir the powder and wait. The advice is that you can put it in the fridge to cool and maybe drink it from a straw when it's ready. It looks a little like wallpaper paste and smells…erm, unnatural.

After 15 minutes, it's time to start. So slowly pour a little into a glass and take your first sip (I can actually taste it thinking about it). Then you take a sip of water and you repeat this over an hour until all the mixture is gone.

I can do that, no problem! I gagged the first sip. I couldn't believe how bad it tasted! It was like I'd been punched in the throat and my tastebuds had been attacked with what I can only describe as a salt snowball. I felt immediately nauseous. I had to compose myself. I knew how vital it was to have the prep in order to have a colonoscopy. Afterall, they were looking for more cancer, for more issues, I needed to get this done.

Right, time for another sip. I nearly spat this out! For some reason I left it in my mouth longer, my body fighting against me, not wanting me to swallow this "stuff".

You have to drink the formula within an hour. That's the instructions and I didn't wanna to fall at the first hurdle, I needed to carry on. Third sip and swallow - yuck. You can't chug it. You can't hold your nose and simply fight through it. It's sodium, it's horrendous, but it has to be done, I've started now… One sip prep, one sip water, you're doing well. Wait one minute and have another sip. It makes you do a little dance straight after as it tastes so bad, the body kinda finding its own ways to deal with it. More sips, trying to drink a bigger gulp this time; for some reason I had forgotten how dreadful it was, no more big gulps!

Take your time. I kept reminding myself why I was doing it. How important it was and it was an important part of the process. Keep going. It takes a real effort fighting the urge for it not to come back up or repeat on you. A little burp. That felt good! I needed that. Big gulp of water. Not much gloopy formula left, I can see the finish line. One hour later it was done. I felt drained. I can't actually believe how tough that was. I felt like I needed a lie down, I was exhausted. The instructions say to drink a litre of water for the next hour.

Time to sit down and wait, to let it do its thing. I waited, nothing happening, have I endured this foul drink for nothing? Let's have some water.

Ten minutes later. Hold on…something IS happening…something…inside! A little gurgle, a few odd noises. Strange MOVEMENT in my stomach. Me thinks I should head upstairs to the toilet as quick as one should in these situations! The gurgles increased with intensity as I grabbed the stair rail, going slowly, but at a pace that meant I would reach the toilet in time!

Now here's the thing - Bowel prep WORKS. Be prepared for four hours back and forth to the bathroom. Without being too graphic, let's say it truly does flush your system out, almost like a tap has been turned on full blast!! That's the best description I'll give and I won't give any more gruesome details! Even when you think you're fully flushed out, nope, surprise! There's still some time to go.

Plus, just remember, you have ANOTHER round of prep to do on the morning of the scan!

One of my best piece of advice? Get the softest water based and biodegradable toilet wipes you can. The constant use of paper in that area will leave you sore!

After time, the bowel prep became a real issue for me. I'd put it on a pedestal where I knew I'd have to drink it in say 5 days' time and every single day that's all I would think about. I couldn't focus on anything else; it was horrible. It really was ruining my days in the lead up. 5 days until prep. 4 days until prep. 3 days until prep. These weren't days anymore; they were a countdown to an event that I didn't enjoy one bit.

I had to stop this. I told myself it's one hour out of my day, yes, it'll be tough, but it's ONE HOUR (the drink that is, not the "flushing of the system!!"). My focus would be on the day after; the prep was for that reason and it's a vital step.

My first bowel prep was for a colonoscopy which revealed polyps in my bowel which would need to be removed. These polyps it would turn out, weren't normal, they were serrated (I'll go into more details about this later). It just shows how vital these scans are, no matter how many tests or appointments you've had, a camera can find things that weren't known before.

Everything I've done has been important to my survival, your instincts kick in, yes, it's all tough, but tough!! You need to do it to survive!

My top tips for bowel prep:

- Have a separate glass of water on standby and mix the solution with some cordial, it honestly helps.
- Buy toilet wipes!! The burn from using paper will not be enjoyable.
- Take your time.
- Stand by - you might not think it's gonna work, but boy it does!
- Get near that toilet!!

TikTok, You Don't Stop!

I really wanted a record of my cancer journey, something to look back on in the future. To remember my feelings and emotions, who was with me, what I did. It would be a cathartic way of not only making sure I journaled what was happening, but to share it with others and let friends know what I was going through daily.

I didn't have TikTok but thought joining this would be the best place to get myself out there. I had to start somewhere. My first upload was describing my cancer, speaking to whoever watched was the plan, describing how I felt, who I am and what it all meant. Of course I wore my leopard print shirt! I felt confident, used my experience of shopping tv to look at the screen, connect with the audience, talk slowly and not waffle. I uploaded it and felt a sense of freedom from putting it out into the universe. My confidence was high; I had achieved what I wanted for the day.

I decided to investigate HAMN a little more, to make more people aware of this one in a million cancer, to connect with others. I wanted to blog my journey in a way that gave hope and a positive vibe. I showed my daily life, my walks, my food, my clothes. I showed my raw emotions…this cancer was real, but it wasn't going to beat or define me.

I had tons of likes and comments, people wanted to connect with me, talk to me about their own cancers, their own experiences. I met people who had beaten cancer, people who were going through cancer, people who had lost loved ones to cancer. I felt a huge empathy towards everyone; I wanted to talk and to help others. This was so empowering to me. Maybe this is what I'm good at, listening and helping?

I can honestly say, it's been one of the best decisions I've ever made. Not only was it a way to get things off my chest and into the universe in a positive way, but it brought a community of people together, strangers who became friends, their kindness gave me power and strength that I didn't know I had, especially in my darkest days. It gave me a voice; I was seen and heard. It allowed my confidence to come back slightly. It allowed me to show that I will not be beaten easily. To the people that became a daily constant in my life and helped me so much - THANK YOU - Chrissy, Mel, Kelly, Susie and Evelyn. There's way more to thank, but these became my constant companions.

My TikTok friends are incredible, they check in on me, share their own stories with me and really do care about me. Mel gave me the confidence to draw. Chrissy made a mug with my drawings on. Susie believed in my art, especially Gertrude the Giraffe. Kelly became invaluable to me after she lost her husband. Evelyn checked in on me daily, always giving me positive vibes. Again, there are so many other connections to thank, so if I haven't named you, know you're on my mind and I'm so grateful for you!

In my lives, I'd created a safe place, a place for people who had been through extremely tough times to come together and chat, to take their minds off the bad days, to smile and embrace life. I felt hope, energy, enthusiasm. I gave an 'up yours' to cancer!

I shared details of my appointments, outcomes, frustrations, hopes, and dreams. I was given a freedom to express myself and connected with others on another level and that empowered me. I was helped so much by strangers who had heard my story so far and who shared their own stories with me. I found solace in listening to others. I enjoyed it. I wanted to help.

TikTok also taught me how precious and fragile life is. There's been many survivors who have reached out to me and have shown me so much kindness and empathy; they tell me how proud they are of me and how well I'm doing. However, there's also the very real and sad side, people who I've spoken to that lost their battle. Those who I shared moments with that I can never do again. It's a powerful and humbling reminder of what I've been through. I continue to this day loading videos on TikTok, sharing insights into my life and my journey.

Clearing Out

Waiting for my operation date was tough. I needed a distraction, a purpose, some focus. I decided I needed a clear out. This is sometimes called nesting. Before a life-changing event you tidy up or clear out, as if preparing yourself, your home. It's true what they say - messy house equals messy mind!

I wasn't a hoarder by any means, but I had kept so many memories from my childhood. Maybe it was a way of clinging to the happy and positive parts of those years? The biggest thing I held onto were my action figures. They weren't just toys; they were my escape from reality. I'd spend hours playing with them, making up stories of heroes and villains, good versus evil.

My mom spent her hard-earned money adding to my collection whenever she could. He-Man was my favourite, but I also had Star Wars, Transformers and Thundercats. The best part was that they could all mix together. A Transformer could fight Skeletor, Luke could team up with Lion-O. They didn't need rules or logic, just imagination. I'd bash them together in battles, line them up on the stairs and throw them down as if they were tumbling from a mountain. Those afternoons gave me an escape. For a little while, everything was simple - good versus bad, and good always had a fighting chance.

Fast forward to now. The clear-out wasn't just about getting rid of old stuff. I also needed money, quickly. I was out of work, living alone with a mortgage and the stress was building daily. My loft was full of boxes and bags, a mountain of my own waiting to be tackled.

I started going through them one by one. There's definitely a market for action figures, but usually only if they're in pristine condition and still in their original boxes. Let's just say mine had been through enough wars that they carried the scars to prove it. Some were missing limbs, weapons or even heads. Others were worn smooth from being handled and played with so much. They weren't collector's items, they were survivors.

I had hundreds. I sorted them into piles. The ones too battered to sell went into one group. The ones that still had a chance went into another. Then I had a pile of strays - a single figure here, a helmet there, a broken laser gun from someone I couldn't even remember. The plan was simple. I'd take decent photos, show the wear and tear honestly, highlight the good parts and write up descriptions. Then I'd put them online and hope for the best.

Things sold quickly, although not always for the prices I'd dreamed of. But money was money and right then that's what mattered. The broken ones surprised me the most. At first, I thought they'd go straight into the bin but then I had the idea to bundle them together as bulk buys, spare parts for collectors, or maybe just oddities for someone else's projects. To my amazement, they sold too! Three bulk lots gone in a matter of days. I was chuffed!

What really surprised me, though, was how it made me feel. I'd expected to feel loss, like I was giving away the last pieces of my childhood. Instead, I felt something entirely different. Joy. I loved holding the figures again, remembering the made-up battles, reliving the afternoons of imagination. And more than that, I loved the thought that other people would get joy from them now. These toys from the 80s carried stories not just for me but for anyone who grew up in that time. Maybe someone else would open the box and be taken straight back to their own childhood.

It gave me focus. Each day I had tasks: take photos, write descriptions, reply to messages, pack and send orders. It was a rhythm. A purpose. And while it might not sound like much, when you're dealing with something like cancer and your mind is spinning with uncertainty, that small sense of control feels like gold.

The whole process taught me something unexpected. Clearing out wasn't really about the toys. It was about me. It was about proving to myself that I could sort through the mess, make decisions and let go without fear. I realised that just because I no longer owned the figures, it didn't mean that I had lost what they had given me. The memories remain. The joy of those afternoons, the stories I created, the comfort they gave me - none of that disappears when the toys leave the loft. In fact, selling them felt freeing, it reminded me that life moves forward; we carry the past with us, but we don't need to stay buried in it. By letting go, I made space for new things, new memories, new chapters.

There was also another layer to it; Those figures had their scars, missing parts, and battle damage, yet they still had value. They still had a story to tell. Just like me. My body carried the scars from my appendectomy. I was still recovering when I was diagnosed with cancer. My life had been through battles, yet I am still here, still standing, still worth something. That parallel didn't escape me. Clearing out wasn't about losing my childhood. It was about reconnecting with it and then using it to step forward. I could look at those figures, smile at what they meant to me and then let them go without sadness, instead of holding on tight to the past. I realised I was stronger for releasing them. Sometimes life feels heavy because we're clinging onto things we no longer need. The act of clearing out gave me space not just in my loft but in my mind. It gave me a sense of purpose at a time when I needed it most. It reminded me that I wasn't starting again empty handed. I had my memories, my resilience and now, a clearer space to build something new.

If you're reading this while facing your own mountain of clutter, whether it's boxes in a loft or feelings weighing you down, I'd say this: Clearing out is more than tidying, it's a way of reminding yourself that you can let go and still be whole.

The toys were gone, but the joy remained. I realised that's exactly what I needed in my life; room for growth, room for joy, room for the future that I still had ahead of me.

Birthday Celebrations

My surgery was in 3 weeks' time. I was so relieved to find out that it wouldn't be before my birthday in case I'd have to spend that day in hospital. I've always made a huge thing about my birthday, whatever job I've had, it's literally the first day I book off, there is no way I'm working on my big day!

My Mom has always made me cakes throughout the years; He-Man's castle Grey Skull when I was 5 was truly incredible! Later, she continued this trend with cakes with themes; Skulls, Dexter and even Game of Thrones!

This year was obviously slightly different. I wouldn't say I felt subdued about celebrating, but I knew the operation wasn't far away, so that would always be in my mind. I wanted to celebrate my birthday with my Mom and then meet some of the lads later that evening. Everyone knew I had cancer and that my surgery was pending. It was a chance to see a few people before the big day, not as a goodbye, but as an 'I'll be ok'.

My Mom has always managed to treat me on my birthdays, no matter how hard times were growing up. She always finds something special for me, something meaningful. This year was no different, a skull mug and 600 bags of Barry's tea! That should last me... well, the way I drink tea, about a month ha! I had tons of presents to open and felt like a kid at Christmas, ripping open the paper to reveal yet another gift. It felt special, *I* felt special.

Emotions were obviously high. We treated it as normally as we possibly could. This was my birthday, so it was a time to celebrate and enjoy the moment. Brave faces were on! I'd bought myself a new shirt, very smart, pale blue, but being me, it still had to have some quirky touches - tigers on the collar, nice! My best aftershave was on (Tom Ford Tobacco Vanille for those wondering!), black cord trousers, black belt and my shiny doc martins, I felt fantastic.

Now, where did I want my celebratory b'day meal to be with my Mom? You guessed it, it had to be a pizza place! Taxi arrived and it was time to go, one last spritz of aftershave very quickly! You never know, the Italian waitress might be flirty!

I ordered my favourite, a simple margarita with black olives, chilli flakes and a ton of extra garlic. Oh, is that truffle oil?! Why not, let's go all out. *"Drinks?"* Oh, go on then, let's have an espresso martini to start and then we can order a nice bottle of red wine. It felt so good to be out of the house, to be dressed up, to go to a restaurant. To celebrate, to feel good about myself and not have to worry or focus on the chaos that being diagnosed with cancer can bring.

The espresso martinis came, and wow they were lovely! The birthday treats had definitely started! Next was the pizzas and red wine, which was truly amazing. Me and my Mom can always chat about anything, random convos about series we've been watching or just general chat about life. It was such a lovely and calm time. A little bit away from reality for at least a few moments.

Pizza finished and time to get my Mom back to hers and for me to meet my mates. I went to a local brewery, but I was so tired. A few beers, a hug from Millsy and a few other of the lads perked me up. However, the strain I'd faced mentally with all the information about my upcoming operation had taken its toll, I was wiped out and needed to go home.

A short taxi ride back, door open, shoes off. Turns out the Villa were on TV, so I ordered a curry, win win! A nice relaxing way to end the day, plus Villa won!

One Week to Go

A week before my operation and everything felt surreal. I wasn't feeling the best. Not just physically, but mentally too. I'd been told to start a low fibre diet. That meant no fruit or vegetables. "Hold on, I'm a vegetarian, so what exactly am I meant to eat?!" The answer, apparently, was white carbs. Usually, I'd be jumping for joy at that suggestion. Pasta, bread, rice, crumpets. But this wasn't the fun version of carbs. This was plain pasta with no sauce, dry cereals, white toast with no seeds or nuts, and crumpets with nothing interesting on them. My plate was beige. Beige breakfast, beige lunch, beige dinner. Food had lost its colour, its texture, its excitement. I hadn't realised how much joy I got just from a crisp bite into an apple, or a plate piled with veg, or even just something as simple as a banana on toast. Now all I had was blandness, carbs stripped of flavour, stripped of identity. I swear, even cardboard would have been more exciting.

The hardest bit was the control. I didn't cheat once, I couldn't. This was far too important. This was the biggest thing in my life. If I messed up, it wasn't just about feeling ill, it was about risking the surgery that would save my life. I couldn't let myself down. I couldn't let my Mom down. So, I ate my beige food, staring at each plate like it was punishment, but necessity.

Throughout the day I fantasised about what I couldn't have. A juicy apple, crunchy broccoli, a salad bursting with colour. It wasn't just food I was missing - it was the life that went with it; That first bite, the sensation of juice spilling out, the crack of a carrot snapping in half and then dipping it in some lovely hummus. Funny how when you're told you can't have something, it suddenly becomes the only thing you want.

It wasn't just the food though. It was the lack of control. I felt like my body wasn't mine anymore. My choices were being taken away one by one. The diet was strict, my routine was dictated by appointments, hospital letters, preparations and surgery was looming whether I wanted it or not. The sense that life was no longer in my hands hit harder than I expected. It was daunting.

I knew I had to pull myself out of this funk. Sitting and overthinking wasn't going to help. What could distract me? A film - that was the answer. Something to pull me out of my own head and into another world for a couple of hours. Horror? Normally my favourite, but no, I didn't fancy it. Gangster films? Another favourite, but again, I wasn't in the mood. Thriller, action, drama? Nothing clicked. Then, after a search, I saw it: *The Naked Gun*. Slapstick, ridiculous, completely daft - that was exactly what I needed! Within seconds I was laughing, not a little chuckle, but full-on laugh out loud every thirty seconds. For the first time in weeks, I felt that buzz of dopamine hit. I laughed until my face hurt and my eyes streamed. For those ninety minutes I wasn't a cancer patient on a strange diet waiting for my stomach to be cut open. I was just a bloke enjoying a silly comedy. A VERY silly comedy.

The next day, I queued up *Naked Gun 2½*. I made a little ritual of it - kettle on, brew in hand, curtains closed, let's make this an event! Same result. Laughter. Joy. Escape. For ninety minutes I was pulled out of my own head and away from the endless "what ifs" that haunted me. Leslie Nielsen was a genius. There will never be another like him.

The day after that - *Naked Gun 33 ⅓*. I rationed them carefully, one a day, like someone rationing chocolate. It gave me something to look forward to. Something silly, ridiculous, yet completely vital. Laughter gave me back a sense of power, it reminded me that I was still me, that I could still laugh. But reality always came back in.

A few days before surgery I had to go in for my pre-assessment. Blood tests, paperwork, checks, and then the big one: A complex polypectomy. They removed nine serrated polyps. Nine. That number stuck with me.

It took an hour and a half to remove them. I'd got changed into my gown and those wonderful paper pants with a hole in the back:

"Yes, the hole is for the camera to go up, so make sure the hole is at the back!"

Oh, I get it, don't worry! I shuffled to the waiting area, paper pants rustling away. I sat down, trying to look casual when really all I wanted to do was disappear. There was another bloke waiting, he was a lot older than me. I found out even at 42, that I was very young for all this to be happening. We caught each other's eye and gave the standard man-nod of acknowledgement. No words needed. We both knew what we were there for.

When they called me in, I lay there on the bed feeling more like a specimen than a person. The nurses were kind, but my nerves were through the roof. I gripped the edge of the bed, holding the sheets and stared at the ceiling tiles. My stomach flipped every so often, not with pain exactly, but with sheer unease. I inhaled as much gas and air as I could, to the point one of them told me to stop, to breathe properly, to calm down. Easy for them to say when they weren't lying there with a camera up their bum!

By the end I was wiped out, exhausted. But I told myself 'this is one more step closer to the surgery that will save your life. One more thing ticked off the list'.

Nighttime was the hardest part of my day. My brain refused to shut off and I'd lie there staring at the ceiling, listening to the creaks of the house, my thoughts racing. What if I didn't wake up from surgery? What if they opened me up and found something more, or something worse? What if the cancer came back? What if, what if, what if? I tried everything; Warm drinks (and not my usual brew), podcasts, calming music, even white noise. Sometimes I'd nod off for an hour, then wake at 3am just staring into the darkness again. I'd hear cars passing down the road, then the birds waking up, then I'd see the faint light sneaking through the curtains. I just lay there knowing I hadn't slept much, but that there was nothing I could do. The tiredness piled on top of everything else and I was drained.

As if that wasn't enough, my car decided to die on me, the battery kept running flat. Some days it would start after three or four attempts, other days it was completely dead. I had to rely on my kind neighbours to jump-start it for me. Without that car I felt trapped. Appointments, shopping, getting to my mom's - all suddenly gone. Eventually, I got the battery replaced at the local garage, pricier than I'd like, but done, relief. Until, a few days later, when it gave up completely. Dead. The key jammed in the ignition. I sat there, staring at the dashboard in disbelief. I tried for ten minutes to get that blooming key out and nothing. Are you being serious? I've got cancer, I'm days away from surgery, and now this? I slammed the door, kicked the tire and nearly broke down completely. It felt like everything was falling apart at once. I'd had enough.

My mind linked it all together. The cancer, the mortgage going up, the car breaking down. It felt like the universe was out to get me, but deep down I knew none of it was connected. My car didn't know I had cancer and my mortgage didn't either. Life was just messy and unfair.

With the key stuck in the ignition, I draped a black towel over the steering wheel, shut the door and hoped for the best. After all, no one could nick it, it couldn't go anywhere! Eventually I found a local electrical engineer. He diagnosed a parasitic drain on the battery; Something in the car was constantly draining power, even when it wasn't running. While he tested and tinkered, I made him a cuppa and we chatted. My cancer came up in conversation. I didn't mean to play the sympathy card, but maybe part of me wanted him to know what I was going through. He told me his ex-wife had died of cancer, a different type he added quickly, but still. That moment of connection mattered. It reminded me that I wasn't alone in this. A few days later he came back, fixed the fault, jump-started the car. Relief doesn't even cover it, for the first time in weeks something had gone right. I got my car back.

The next few days blurred. I tried to fill them with little routines. Films, walks when I had the energy, cups of tea at my Mom's house. That was my safe place, sitting in her living room with a brew, sometimes talking openly about my cancer, sometimes not, just being there, just being with her.

I cleaned the kitchen, tidied the living room, even did the washing up. I hate tidying, but there was no way I was coming back from surgery to a mess - or worse, my Mom cleaning up after me. That simply wouldn't be fair! I thought about the operation in minute detail; The scar I was about to get, how my body would never look the same again, how my life would never *be* the same. Sometimes I stood in front of the mirror, tracing my stomach, wondering what it would look like with a fresh scar running down it. Would I still recognise myself?

That week taught me something important. Fear doesn't just live in the big things. It creeps into your diet, your sleep, your broken-down car. But so does hope. Hope sneaks in through a silly film, a neighbour's kindness, a stranger fixing your car, a quiet cuppa at your Mom's. The week before surgery was chaos, but in that chaos, I found lifelines.

If you're facing something similar, my advice is this: find your *Naked Gun;* Find that thing that makes you laugh, that takes you out of your own head for a while; Let people help you; Accept the kindness of friends, family, neighbours, nurses, whoever crosses your path. Focus on the little victories - a decent brew, a little walk, a good night's sleep, seeing your Mom, because those little victories build up. They remind you that you're still here, still fighting, still living. And sometimes that's enough to get you through the longest week of your life.

The Day Before Surgery

I woke up early and weirdly felt quite excited! It was almost time. The last three months had been relentless. Three months, that's all it had been but it had felt like three years. Appendix burst, cancer diagnosis, meeting my specialist, two colonoscopies and now my surgery. I'd been through so much in a short space of time. This had become my life, cancer was all I thought and talked about, every single moment, every single day encapsulated by cancer. Now, all of a sudden, here I was, the day before surgery. It's weird how it has crept up on me. I vividly remember saying on TikTok "operation in 19 days' time" and then bam, it was now only a day away.

It was a Sunday. Breakfast was by 9am and then I had to do my bowel prep at 2pm and 6pm. This became the days format and process for me to follow. For some reason this prep wasn't as bad as the others, maybe it felt like some small sense of control? I had a structure and I knew the outcome would meet my expectations. I was in a good space mentally.

Next, let's pack my hospital bag. An over the shoulder bag that I've used for holidays - but this was definitely no vacation away! This was not a beach holiday; there would be no pina coladas or siestas. This was it, life changing, major surgery. First, my leopard print dressing gown, some funky pj's, a book (A Clockwork Orange), toiletries, inhalers, tablets, headphones, bits and bobs - all the essentials I needed. I knew I'd be in hospital for at least a week, if I needed anything else, my Mom could always bring it. I felt calm whilst packing, grounded and ready.

Again, it was part of the process, mental preparation and something to tick off the list.

The sun was shining, so I decided to go out for a nice walk. One last bit of fresh air and nature before my surgery. I wasn't sure how long my recovery would be, so I better get some exercise! I took myself to Cannon Hill Park, a historic and glorious park with huge woods, geese, ducks, swans, and even herons. There's a wonderful nature centre, a theatre, lakes - it's such a fantastic place and it's always had a kind of magic for me, like a patch of countryside planted in the middle of the city.

It was a beautiful day - subtle breeze, bright blue skies dotted with fluffy white clouds. It was picturesque, perfect walking weather. I kept a slow pace, taking it all in, taking my time to embrace nature. I walked through the woods, listening to the leaves rustle in the wind, feeling each step, I took, hearing the birds chirp away. I felt safe in my sanctuary.

Now into the park area that winds and twists around various little lakes. Sundays can be pretty busy there. It's a popular spot, so I knew there would be people on bikes, groups of runners etc that I'd try to avoid. Hold on - there's more runners than usual…and they have numbers pinned on and are wearing PINK. It was the cancer fun run. The day before my operation and I decided to go to this park at this time, not knowing the event was on. I stood there stunned.

The synergy I felt, the connection, was the universe telling me all will be ok? I was emotional but focussed, this was amazing! I smiled at the runners; I smiled because it felt so energising and powerful for me. I needed to see this today. All these runners for doing it for a cause, for cancer.

Maybe they'd faced it themselves and overcome it, maybe they were going through it right now, a friend, a family member, maybe they'd lost someone. It gave me a sense of ease, a sense of community; ALL these pink tops, running in the park today wanted to focus their energy on cancer awareness and raise money. I felt so positive. It was almost like all of this was for me!

I got home after an hour, no cups of tea allowed so I was stuck with water. My mind was focussed, I felt ready, emotionally and physically. This was happening. All the preparations, the appointments, it was all coming to a close very soon.

I remember sitting in the quiet, trying to absorb the stillness. It was strange - my life was about to change forever, yet the house was calm…ordinary. I can't even remember what I did with the rest of the day. Did I watch TV? Listen to music? Just sit there in silence? It's a blur. Maybe my brain has filed it away to protect me.

What I do remember is this: the last glass of bowel prep, job done. I set my alarm for 6:30am. The ritual of plugging my phone in, laying it beside me. Ear plugs in. A quiet sense of ease. I lay there, staring at the ceiling, knowing tomorrow was the biggest day of my life. That my body would be opened up and altered forever. Weirdly, I wasn't afraid. I was ready.

Let's do this!

21st May 2024 - The Big Day

I woke up with a smile. It was a conscious decision to do this, to smile, to feel good, to keep focussed, stay strong and stay happy. The sun was shining. **Positive vibes only**. Quick shower. No breakfast allowed before surgery. Dressed and ready to go.

My best mate Millsy picked me up at 7am, it felt like some fun road trip that we used to go on. But alas, this was no adventure. We then picked up my Mom and off to the hospital we went. A half an hour's drive, I kept the spirits high, I wanted my Mom to know that I was ok. She needed to see me ready for the big fight, ready to give it my all and beat this. My Mom smiled and nodded, but her hands were tight in her lap, highlighting what she was really feeling. She's always been strong, but no mother should ever have to take her child to surgery like this. She remained fairly quiet for the whole journey.

Millsy dropped us off and left after a big manly hug. Just me and my Mom now. We went to the waiting area and it wasn't too long before my name was called. Off into a little side room just for me; Doctors, nurses, anaesthetists, surgical assistants all came through one by one. Forms signed, checked, double-checked, triple checked. Everyone calm, professional, efficient. I liked it - the busyness made the time fly. I felt good. Focused. Ready. Like a boxer sitting in the corner of the ring, gloves on, robe over my shoulders, bouncing my legs while the crowd roared. This was my fight.

By 9:30am I was told to get changed into my hospital gown and pop on those beautiful paper pants, hardly my

Calvin's! Next, put my dressing gown on over the top, ready to go to surgery. Of course, I had my trusty fluffy leopard print dressing gown with me. That gown was more than clothing; it was part of my armour. If I was going into battle, I was going in with style! I hugged my Mom tight and told her "Love you" and "see you soon." She clung on for just a second longer than usual, eyes tearing up but steady. Her strength in that moment was everything. It was nearly time for the main event. The biggest event in my life.

I assumed a porter would wheel me down to surgery, but no, I would be walking. So, there I was, striding through the hospital in paper pants and a leopard print dressing gown, heading for the operating theatre. People stared and laughed, I gave them a grin, almost that embarrassed "oh well" look. The nurses loved it. That was the point; If I could make people smile, even for a second, then I wasn't just another patient walking to theatre, I was *me*. I wasn't going glum. Positive energy and positive vibes!

Then came the anaesthetic room. Things felt different here. Bright lights, sterile white walls, machines humming, trays lined with shiny metal instruments. At the far end facing me, the double doors into theatre loomed. They looked humongous! Like the gates of something ancient and serious. I caught myself staring at them, thinking that's where it happens*, **that's where my life changes forever.***

I didn't have time to focus on that. Gown off, things were getting serious now. We spoke again about what would happen and checked over the forms *again* confirming that I was still happy to have this surgery: "Yes, I want the surgery".

Suddenly, it got a little quieter, almost a calm before the storm. The team were gearing up, prepping. First thing was a small injection into my lower back, a "bee sting", albeit a VERY painful bee sting! Sharp and mean it almost burnt. Now I had to lean forwards slightly for my epidural; I was slumped over waiting for the injection to work. I stayed quiet as the world continued closing in a little. I was asked by the team if I was ok. I felt emotional, butterflies in my stomach, was this actually happening? Reality had set in: "I'm ok…it's just all become real". A comforting hand then rested on my shoulder letting me know they were there for me.

Next, epidural - I felt it - so needed another bee sting may be needed, ouch!

"Let's wait five more minutes."

Another epidural now. That was an interesting one as I didn't "feel" it as such, but it felt a little rough, like I just knew something was happening. It's hard to explain the sensation but it was done and now I could lie back.

Then it's a little blurry, you're lying there, waiting; 'Try to relax', emotions are high, 'don't cry'. Even writing this I feel emotional. 'Things can and do go wrong'…no, get that out your head, this team is incredible, you have one of the best surgeons in the country. You'll be FINE.

Cannula in. Now for the anaesthetist to work his magic. I think I was injected and then given a mask, maybe with oxygen. I'm not sure if I was told to count down from ten or just to relax and let it happen, but this was it, time to go to sleep and have my surgery. Off I went, drifted away…

The next thing I remember I was awake, still in the anaesthetic room. Hold on, I've had my surgery! Was that it? Had it happened? Did it go ok? The anaesthetist explained the surgery HAD happened, that I needed to be transported to recovery and Mr Shariff would be round shortly to talk to me. Major surgery done. I'm ALIVE.

I was ever so carefully and gently moved to EPOC (Enhanced Post Operative Care), a specialist critical care unit who would monitor and look after me.

I was transferred from the op bed to another bed via a backboard. I had about 12 tubes in me. Then, I saw my Mom, I smiled and she smiled back. I felt ok, awake, compos mentis. I'd done it, I'd survived.

Mr Shariff came to the bedside and told me everything had gone well and to plan. Second thing he told me was that he didn't cut into my death head tattoo on my sternum (shows his humour!). The third thing he said was that I didn't need a stoma, phew! I had been so worried about that, I think that one extra thing could've been a real struggle for me mentally. He assured me that he was able to successfully reattach my bowel together after removing 30%. He left to allow me to rest. His job was done.

My Mom stayed for a while, we held hands, it felt great that it was over! I'm not sure what we actually spoke about. I couldn't move, so she had to adjust her chair because I wanted to see her face. It was a really long day for her as well. I'd essentially had the easier part, going to sleep and having the surgery, whilst she'd had to wait, worry, think. She's so strong and I can't image how hard and painful counting down the minutes and hours was, waiting for a phone call and not knowing if the news would be good or bad. She's such an amazing person.

My Mom left after a little while to allow me to rest. My body had taken a beating, a huge traumatic event. I think I was in and out of consciousness for a few hours. The EPOC team introduced themselves, they were a two-to-one care facility, checking in on me, making sure I was ok. Incredible and lovely people. The checks were done for the night but every now and then I'd wake whilst more were done, but for the majority, I was out of it. Drained and wiped out but overall, relieved.

EPOC (Enhanced Post Operative Care)

I woke up feeling, well, pretty positive, a bit groggy but I'd done it! I had survived the operation!

The care in EPOC was incredible. Every team member was attentive; they cared, smiled and truly wanted to help with my recovery. They looked after my every need, it wasn't simply doing the required checks or tests, they wanted to know how I was feeling and would reassure me that I was doing well. When the evening came, the team changed hands but the care was still as attentive, more big smiles, more positive vibes. They were so warming and that gave me strength.

I had about 12 tubes in me from surgery - three in my neck, a feeding tube, a blood drain, my Ryles tube, a cannula in my hand, a cannula in my arm, another cannula in my wrist, an A-line (artery line), a catheter and maybe a few others I can't remember!

The Ryles tube basically went up my nose, down my throat and into my stomach. Its job was to remove gas, fluids, or toxins from the stomach. After two days it was decided to remove the Ryles tube to see how I got on. Well, I didn't get on very well! Extreme pain, bloating, sweating, temperature spiking. "Ok, let's get that tube back in." Now, the original Ryles tube was put in whilst I was out cold in surgery. To get it back in, I'd be awake while the nurse fed 60cm of, not the thinnest tube, up my nose, down my throat and into my stomach. The prospect did not sound good at all! I was given a glass of water with a straw and clear instructions:

"Keep sipping on the straw and keep swallowing".

I needed a moment of composure. A deep breath and then "I'm ready". Sip of water, swallow, sip of water, swallow. Only focussing on the sips and swallows as I got a tube slid into my nose. Sip, swallow, more tube going in, up, then down my throat and into my stomach. It didn't actually take too long before it was in, connected, and taped to my nose. Another job done.

Next, let's discuss the A-line in my wrist - straight into the artery, which sounded pretty scary! On the third day in EPOC, it was time for it to come out. My Mom was there visiting, by my side. Out of the 10 days I was in hospital, she only didn't come one day and that's because I had friends visit me. What a superstar she truly is! Anyway, where was I? Oh yes, the A-line needed to come out of my wrist, yuck. I was nervy as the nurse began, then out it popped and blood started gushing! The nurse quickly put pressure on it and we both smiled, I mean, what better place to be than in hospital for this kinda thing eh? Plus, I'd just had the biggest surgery they could do, this was nothing! More pressure applied for about a minute, *"let's have a look"*, nope, still bleeding! In these sorts of situations, you just have to sit and let them do their job! No pressure, no panic, we were all calm. It stopped bleeding after a few minutes and was all good!

The EPOC team washed me, took care of me. Kept me safe and comfortable. Every check was carried out with precision. I had encouragement throughout the day and I was made to feel special.

Let's Get Physical, Physical!

Day 1 - The day after my surgery, two Physiotherapists came to get me up at 10:30am. Hold on, were they serious? I've just had a major operation! However, I soon realised that they were more than serious. The quicker you get up, the quicker you heal, FACT! Ok, fair enough, if this is what happens, let's go for it.

They were super friendly, explaining what their role was and what they'd like to see me achieve. There was a clear guide set out for me, simple steps to get me ready to eventually go home.

"Right, let's get those legs moving, wiggle your left toes"

…done.

"Raise your left leg"

… tricky but done.

"Now the right side"

…erm, not happening, can't feel a thing. What was going on? A cold spray came out, first on my arm to show the sensation (bloomin' freezing) then on my left foot…freezing, left leg…freezing, slightly higher…cold, left side of my stomach…nowt. Right toes…nothing, right leg…nothing, upper leg…cold, stomach…FREEZING. It turns out the epidural had moved, meaning it had essentially stopped the feeling in my leg rather than my operation site, nothing worrying after all!

Right, that was out the way. The next task was to sit up, I used my hands to prop myself up and wiggle, very very slowly up the bed. My eyes were shut tight, concentrating.

"Paul, open your eyes".

"I can't, I'm trying!" For some reason they just shut themselves tight, almost in protest to what my body was trying to do! I guess it's like the way you turn down the radio in the car to "see" better when parking!

Eventually one eye opened to a squint, then the other and ever so slowly they opened fully. Now, the task of simply sitting up wasn't easy. Think of your core and how the muscles tightens when you get up; My core had been opened wide and then stapled back up just 18 hours ago. Sitting up is something you do without thinking, innate, part of everyday life. But life had changed and this was the first time I had to sit up after my major operation.

It was daunting but I was determined. I'd been given a task, my first one, and I wasn't going to fail. Let's grab onto the physio's arm for help. Let's take it as slow as possible. Inch by inch I moved up, slowly, calmly, methodically. Ok, I'm sat up! Wow! It was incredibly tough and draining, but I'd managed it. The physios were happy too; it was huge progress the day after my surgery and that meant so much. As I couldn't feel or move my right leg, that was more than enough for today. They said their goodbyes and would return the next day.

Day 2 - Today's challenge was to sit up and get to the edge of the bed, challenge accepted! Again, there's no rush, the physio's arm was offered for support if I needed it. I took my time. I knew the sensation and feeling from yesterday. I started to wiggle up the bed, then stopped. I needed rest, that's OK…Let's wiggle a little more and then I started to use my hands to raise myself up to a sitting position, done. Next, the hard part, to work my way to the edge of the bed, swing my legs, and creep forward bit by bit. The physio pointed to a chair:

"That's where we want to get you, in that chair".

Ok, deep breath. I got to the edge of the bed: "I think that's it. I can't do anymore". And you know what? That was absolutely fine. It was a monumentous effort to get to the edge of the bed. Now, I just had to get back!

Day 3 - The chair. Oh, you know it's happening today! That chair had been staring at me all morning. It seemed like a mile away but was only a few metres. I've already mentioned that I'm stubborn, and when I'm set a task, I want to win. Not for anyone else, but for me. For my own pride, my own self-belief, to know that I CAN do the thing. Maybe from a young age I was told I couldn't, I failed, I wasn't going to achieve anything. Well, guess what, today I WILL! There is no can't in my vocabulary today!

Wiggle, use hands, sit up, swing legs, get to the edge of the bed. Now stand up. Ok, I'm a little wobbly, that's fine, it's my first time stood up since the op. Let's take a little sit down on the edge of the bed again. Both physios were there, ready to help me if I needed them, and I had complete trust in them.

Ok, round two. Stand up slowly. Nice. One foot in front of the other - I'm walking! A few more steps, turn around slowly and sit. I'd done it!

"Excellent work! How do you feel?"

"I feel pretty good! This seats comfy!" The physios weren't just there to tick a box on a sheet, to get me from A to B and say, cool, see you tomorrow. No, they were there to build my confidence up. To make me feel more powerful, and that I could achieve these goals, no matter how hard they initially felt.

Now, back to the bed. They had to do this to make sure I could manage it. Done. I felt fantastic. I could see the progress there and then. I could look at that chair, almost like a mountain in the distance and say to myself, I conquered that.

Day 4 - Time for a walk. The Physios came to the ward, but to their surprise, my bed was empty. I was sat in the chair waiting for them, smiling from ear to ear! The smiles were mirrored back; I'd managed to get up and out my bed and sat in the seat by myself. Now, it's worth noting, I didn't rush this progress. I also let the nurses know that I was going to do it. In recovery, there's no rush, you're not on anyone else's timescale apart from your own. Take your time, listen to your body.

It was time for a walk. Tubes needed disconnecting from this machine and from that machine. I had to carry one of those metal poles on wheels that you always see in hospital dramas. My task was "let's walk as far as you're comfortable with". Ok, let's start. Again, slowly, one foot in front of the other. It felt good, natural. I walked past the nurse's station, all to their glee and surprise!

"You're doing so well!"

I kept going, into the corridor now. I could see the doors to EPOC.

"Do you want to keep going?"

"Yes!" I felt fine, but I was mindful that I did have to get back as well. I made it to the doors, had a little look down the corridor, at the end, there was a sign that said 300-metres. "Can I go there?" I asked. *"Let's try."*

Now, remember, this was my aim, my target, but if I didn't reach it, I hadn't failed at all. Recovery isn't about failure, it's about trying to achieve, step by step goals, not rushing, not risking. If you try, you're already winning and that's half the battle done.

Each step felt fantastic. My posture improved, my mood improved. The 300-metre sign that had seemed 300 miles away was getting closer, and closer, and closer. With every step I was reminded by the physios how well I was doing and that they were there with me. Soon, I placed my hand on the sign and left it there for a few seconds, a very symbolic action. I achieved it, I'd done it. I felt a sense of achievement, full of emotion. Now all I had to do was get back! This was fine, I felt strong, confident. The walk did me well and reminded me that I could get through this. Yes, very simply - one step at a time.

Day 5 - 300 meters to the end of the corridor, been there, done that! Not rushing, I took it slowly, reached that sign and then asked to go further, the 500-metre sign. Walking took me back to a time before the operation, before cancer, before all of this. Walking was my solace, my peace, my safety.

"Where've you been?!" The nurse on the desk gleefully asked. It was amazing to hear the joy in her voice, I felt part of the community, like they were willing me on to complete my marathon. Oh, how I needed a brew though! Unfortunately, that would have to wait a few days.

Day 6 - The final test, stairs. This was the last target before I could be signed off from physiotherapy. Again, I took my steps very slowly, carefully, placing them with precision, this was definitely something that couldn't be rushed. I felt in control; each step was a step closer to my recovery. I managed to get up and down those stairs without any issues. I wanted to do it again whilst they were with me. Again, no issues. I'd "passed" with flying colours. The physio team were super impressed and remarked how well I'd done. what an achievement!

The next day I decided to continue with my walks, keep the blood flowing and keep progressing. Part of me was slowly coming back. There's power in seeing that, feeling that.

Recovery on The Ward

The unpleasant part of my hospital stay. On day 4, I was moved to the general ward, something which turned out to be a horrible experience. I had the biggest cancer operation that hospital does; A huge undertaking, specialist teams that understand the complexities of cancer, the rarity of HAMN and the use of HIPEC - which at the time, could only be done in four hospitals in the country. I was cared for and looked after so gently and incredibly well in EPOC, they smiled, checked in on me and made me as comfortable as possible. They made me feel welcomed and like a human that has gone through the biggest ordeal of their life.

I expected more of the same. I expected to be placed on a specialist cancer recovery ward. My expectations were not met, not by any means.

It was time to be transferred, everyone said their goodbyes to me, with huge smiles and wishes of *"good luck"*. A porter came; the nurses undid all the vital tubes from the wall and placed them on my bed carefully. "CLICK!" The wheels to the bed were unlocked and off we went.

It wasn't too far to go, but in terms of care, it was a million miles away. Ok, maybe that's a little harsh, some were amazing. Mr Dattani, a consultant surgeon checked in on me every day and was fantastic. He worked 9 days straight and always had time for me. He willed me to progress and get better.

Some of the nurses were also brilliant, running around, making sure everyone was ok. The care team were great, singing, dancing, making everyone smile. The day and night shift, were, well night and day. Daytime was extremely busy, tons of people, smiles, chats, banter! The nighttime however, kinda felt like I'd been abandoned it was eerie, uncomfortable and it didn't feel right.

It was hard to sleep with the beeping of machines, some people moaning, others snoring. I needed to rest and couldn't. I always associate things with scenes I've seen in a film. This made me feel like I was in One Flew Over the Cuckoo's Nest; I wasn't a person, I was bed number blah, blah, blah. It felt like I didn't matter at a time I needed to matter the most.

Recovery takes time, there isn't anything else to do on the ward. You are in there to rest, so rest whenever you can.

Seeing The Scar for The First Time

Mr Dattani came to see me on his rounds, checking up on me as usual. I think he found some sort of affinity with me; I was the only one on the ward that had undergone a major operation. Right, time to check the wound site. The bandage came off.

"It's looking good, let's leave it to breathe, in fact, let's leave the bandages off now".

Fantastic news, plus, now I could have a little look! After he went, I gave it a good inspection, well, as much as I could. The scar was bigger than I imaged, it went from the top of my abdomen, around my belly button and further down. That's fine, the operation was huge, the biggest that hospital did.

I counted the staples, 54 in total - wow that's LOADS! They hurt to touch. There was dried blood on my stomach and the scar was odd, the staples sorta squeezed it in like some sort of wiggly worm trying to escape. I tried to take a picture of it so I could take a closer inspection. I studied it, looked in more detail. It intrigued me. This was me now, this was my stomach.

My belly was smooth; I'm not hairy by any means, but obviously they had shaved it. I didn't feel sad or scared of the scar, it was my lifeline, this is what it had taken to have the operation. I felt proud of it. It was a war wound that highlighted what I'd been through and overcome.

The day after, the "blood drain" was removed. This thick tube was connected to a little bag, basically collecting any residual blood that may have been present from the operation. Now, spoiler alert if you're squeamish, blood drains aren't exactly fun to remove. It was the thickest tube on my body. To remove it? The nurse simply pulled it out! It made a sort of gloopy sound and I felt every part of it as it was removed. Yuck! But…another tube gone!

In hospital your ego and inhibitions go - you're vulnerable. You're naked under the gown. You get prodded and poked and don't ask why. They take your temperature, your blood, your blood pressure. Bodily functions are on show. You have to find the funny side!

I was a lot younger than the other patients on the ward, so I guess I connected a little more with the nurses. Granted, I was still about 20 years older than some of them!

One of the nurses that came by daily spoke about how she wanted to move into the theatres and that she's seen a cytoreductive surgery live, spending hours watching the surgeon. It intrigued her, obviously this was the operation I'd just had.

"There are videos on YouTube of it if you want to watch"

Not my actual operation, but others. I just wasn't ready. In fact, it would take me about 3 months before I delved deeper, looking into cytoreductive surgery and HIPEC, researching what actually happens. But for now, I just couldn't face it, it was too soon after the fact. My brain couldn't take any in more information. It was too overwhelming and maybe I simply didn't want to accept the truth that it had just happened to me.

In recovery I faced a number of issues. My temperature spiked several times, meaning more checks, more medications, more poking and more prodding. It would always calm down, but it's things like that do worry you.

One of my worst experiences was with a nurse who I complained about. I won't go into too much depth, however, my Ryles tube was meant to be aspirated (emptied via a syringe) every four hours as requested by the consultant. The Ryles tube is to drain the gas and other nasties and for me, they built up in my stomach more than they expected, so it was vital to keep on top of this. In her 12-hour shift I saw this nurse once, taking my temperature. I'd had a really restless day and I'd closed my curtains to shut myself off and try to rest. I'd already had an issue with her the previous night when she told me that I'd had too much morphine; you can't, the button only allows you so much at a time - common knowledge eh?! Anyway, I didn't want to see her, but she still had her job to do, she had a duty of care. As I was in and out of consciousness and sleep, I didn't really think much of it. I was finally resting; I finally had some peace and felt some relief that I didn't see her.

The next day I woke up in sweats, extreme pain and bloating. I could hardly move; I grabbed onto my bed rail as tightly as I could and managed to press the buzzer. The early shift had come on. The bag for my Ryles tube was full, hard because of all the gas. A consultant was called, trusty Mr Dattani who was fuming, he would not stand for this. Duty of care was missed; he would look into it for me.

The bag was emptied and I felt instant relief but still needed pain medication, anti-sickness, extra care and to be monitored more closely throughout the day. That day, I needed resolution, retribution as it were. This act could've seriously harmed me, harmed my recovery, set me back, given me more time in hospital and away from home. I would not take that. I've always been good at standing up for myself, for what I believe in. I have a code, an honour, I believe in right and wrong and that people should be treated well and nicely. Justice was needed.

I went to the matron's office, yes, there's still matrons! I voiced my concern. My anxiety was on high alert. Was she doing this on purpose? Then, my paranoia kicked in, was she trying to harm me? I was angry, in pain, upset. The matron and head nurse listened. Asked me what I'd like to do; if I'd like to leave it with them or log an official complaint. Now, I have real empathy with nurses and the NHS. Most are incredible, working all hours, seeing pain and suffering every day, but working through it with real compassion and care. This was different though. This directly affected my health and recovery. This affected ME. I wanted it to be official. There was no way I wanted anything else, there needed to be accountability. Luckily, I never saw that nurse again during my time there.

Other issues would take place. The tubes in my neck would get snagged constantly. I was so paranoid about this; what if it came out and I simply bled out there and then?! I've just survived the operation, but will this be how it ends? With every check I'd hold on to that tube, highlighting the point that it would get caught. I couldn't rest, every few hours I would be prodded, poked, blood taken, temp take etc, you simply cannot recover well like that. My thoughts ran back to EPOC again, I missed their care, their compassion. I missed being looked after.

I was unable to eat anything for 8 days. For 6 of those days, it was due to my temperature spiking and my Ryles tube - I was still producing too much nastiness in my stomach. There were slight concerns, but only concerns, nothing to worry about.

Before being offered the food bag, I pointed out that I'm a vegetarian, so I politely asked the question: "Just out of interest, what's in the liquid food?" Apparently, no one had really asked before, so they investigated for me. The liquid meal contained chicken feathers in it (seriously!!). Even Mr Dattani was shocked and appalled, he said if he was in my shoes he'd refuse to have it too. There was no vegetarian option, I found this absolutely ridiculous and disgraceful that they were unable to cater for me, especially in this day and age. How can chicken feathers hold any nutritional value?! This just held up as another annoyance and frustration I found in my care.

One day my leg started to spasm and I felt like I was going to pass out. My Mom was visiting and I'm sure it wasn't a pleasant experience for her to see me like that. Nurses came, then a doctor, curtains shut. I could kinda see a gap in the curtain and I was trying to catch my Mom's eye to make her realise I'd be ok. The leg spasms would last 14 hours. It wasn't a reaction to any medication, it was simply my body asking, "what the hell has just happened here?". A reaction that wouldn't be the last.

I was sick of wearing a hospital gown in bed at night. I needed some sort of normality, some sort of cool clothing. Oh wait, you packed some pj's! I had some dark blue satin ones with bees all over; that's right, even my pj's are funky! I was super careful with all the tubes, making sure not to catch anything. No catheter in anymore (I hated that thing) so I could put my own clothes on now. I had a quick wash and felt fresher, more like myself. Time to get into the bed, which was slightly raised at an angle and had two pillows to help with all the tubes and nasty gas in my stomach. However, I wouldn't be feeling fresh for too long.

I developed night sweats and when I finally did sleep, I'd wake up absolutely drenched, cold sweat, sheets soaking - this would happen 3 times per night. I was extremely tired, stressed, overthinking. The first night I'd worn my own bloody clothes and now they were wringing wet!

I needed to know what was happening; again, paranoia, anxiety, I was worried. One of the surgical team came to see me, reassuring me that my body has been through major trauma, it's confused and is trying to cope, it's "normal". My body wasn't shutting down; it was reacting to the unknown.

Getting my sheets changed at night was a nightmare, some nights only one or two nurses would be on the wards covering 30 plus beds, I know it's not their fault. However, in that situation, in that time of no rest, no sleep, no food, I couldn't cope. I felt lost, uncared for, alone and abandoned. I couldn't believe what I'd been through wasn't as high a priority for them as it was for me. I buzzed and buzzed again. Nothing. I was cold, wet, frustrated and exhausted. I felt weak, like a child who's just wet the bed, almost embarrassed to ask for help. This wouldn't have happened in EPOC - that's what I kept telling myself. I decided to get up and make my way to the nurse's desk. To my surprise, there WAS a nurse there: "Please can you help me?? I'm soaking wet and I've been pressing the buzzer; I just need my sheets changed".

They were busy, I get that, the NHS is overrun and understaffed. But, in that moment, I wasn't just a bed number, another patient. I'd been through the biggest thing in my life. I wasn't one of the old boys who stayed 24 hours after a hernia operation. I'd had CANCER.

I wanted compassion. I wanted care. I wanted the simplicity of getting my sheets changed. I stood soaking wet, undignified, searching for help. Even writing this out now it hurts, I'm annoyed, I'm angry. Reliving these moments is tricky, but I want my story told. Eventually, another nurse came. Rushing about with sheets, giving me a new gown to get changed into.

Two hours later, it happened again. I lay in the cold, wet bed, staring into the darkness. My curtains were closed as I needed sanctuary, to hide, to escape. I didn't know what to do, stay still and hopefully drift off, or buzz and get let down once more. Yes, the what ifs were back. Your mind plays so many evil tricks on you that you question everything.

One of the day nurses told me *"if you need help, use the buzzer, that's what it's for"*. Well, in that case, I'm pressing that buzzer again. This time the nurse came quicker, calmer and more smiley. I felt guilty. Yes, GUILTY for how I'd judged them.

Sheets changed, let's try to rest at last. Ear plugs in, eye mask on, let's block out as much as I can. My night sweats lasted fourteen nights in total, even whilst I was in the comfort of my own bed.

7am, *"Breakfast!! Who wants a cup of tea?"* Well, I do, but I can't! Every single bed around me got a drink while I just got my top up of water. They got to choose their breakfast, cereals, toast, crumpets, even a little biscuit to enjoy with their morning cuppa. I got nothing. I resented them, I felt angry. They didn't know or care what I was going through, they just munched through their breakfast, some complaining, some saying how good it was. I hadn't had much sleep, which obviously affects your mood.

7am you're woken up for breakfast, the lights turn on brightly, the noise of the shift change happening, curtains opening, other patients moving about.

8:30am, the consultants come round, so it's not like you can miss this, you need information and updates.

10:30am, bloods taken.

11am, temperature and blood pressure. Somewhere in between all of this are tablets, injections, morphine and anything else!

12noon, LUNCH! Again, I'd miss out and have to watch everyone else tuck in.

1pm, a visit from my Mom, instantly bringing a smile to my face. She'd leave about 3pm, but again, during those two hours there would be more examinations, checks and the like.

Initially, it was thought that I'd be in the hospital for 7-8 days. However, I'd had no movement in my bowels which can be a real issue once you've had major bowel surgery with reconstruction. I hadn't had a stoma attached, however, I was informed that if no movement happened, then this may have to be an option. Mr Dattani would ask me daily *"any movement?"* When I'd shake my head in response, he'd reply *"dammit!"*.

By Day 8 it was becoming concerning, during the consultant checks I just asked would it not be best if I started some light food, like give my body at least something in order to prompt said movement. I was put on a "sloppy diet", basically wet food, so soup. He noted that he would be in surgery all day, so best of luck to me. Later on that day…hold on, we have a little rumble.

Movement at last. Not much, but it counted. It counted because it showed that my body was responding, healing. My bodily functions were working with some normality. Without that, I would not have been able to leave the hospital and go home safely.

Dr Dattani returned to the ward to check in on me; yes, even after a full day's surgery he wanted to know how I was. I gave him a thumbs up and he punched the air in glee.

The next day he told me that I could go home tomorrow and to make sure I have more movement today. He wouldn't be in the day I was discharged but wished me all the best.

Time To Go Home

I was in hospital for ten days in total and lost a stone in weight. I'd really been through it mentally and physically. I'd changed. Some changes were clear to see, some not so clear.

Today was finally time to go home. I needed to, I'd had enough of that place and the timing felt right. I got up early, excited, but slightly nervous. I didn't really know what the plans would be for the day, what time I would be able to go home etc.

First things first, time for a tidy up. I went to the shower room with my little wash bag, my clothes and my towel. Let's use the hand shower. I'd been using this for the last few days, knowing that I could stand up, but needing to support myself on a rail to wash myself.

Next, let's shave this head! I've been bald for a few years, so nothing to do with my cancer treatment! Once I shave my head, I feel more free, almost like a symbolic removal of something that's weighed me down. Right, now it's time for a beard trim; not too much off, just a little less raggedy.

A little spruce up, some aftershave on and my clothes. Wow, this was the first time I'd put on this particular t-shirt since before the operation and it was a little baggy; man, I've lost some weight! However, when I looked in the mirror and it was me staring back, I smiled. The simplicity of having a refresh meant more than just a shower; it was a reset, leaving the hospital, preparing to go home. It was part of feeling and looking like myself again. No more hospital gowns, no more patient in bed…whatever it was!

7am - the ol' breakfast call, but guess what, I was allowed today! The "sloppy diet" was still in effect, but cereals and a brew were fine. Some normality gained back at last. I think I may even have had a biscuit and some ice-cream.

The consultants came on their rounds at 8:30am. One that I'd not met before; he looked over my notes. He knew the serious nature of the operation that had taken place 10 days before. He wished me well and was happy to know I was headed home.

One of the carers came to my bedside, she knew I was going home. The last few days she'd kept me entertained, singing and dancing, talking about all her exploits in the discos in the late 70's and 80's, she was hilarious! She gave me a hug goodbye and told me not to come back ha!

Before I could go, there was one last thing to face. The tube in my neck. That dreaded line had been with me the whole time, feeding in fluids, drugs, everything I'd needed to keep me going. The thought of it being pulled out terrified me - would it hurt? Would it bleed? I felt my stomach tighten as the head nurse came over. She was calm, steady, she'd done this a *"thousand times"*. I laid down on my side and then in a matter of seconds, done. No blood. No drama. Just gone. The relief was unreal. That was the last tie between me and the hospital.

Then came the goodbyes that mattered the most. I'd made sure that my Mom had bought me some presents for the staff and cards. What present you ask? Well, it's gotta be chocolates of course! I dropped them off at the desk and then walked round to EPOC.

They were my first carers, my safety net, the ones who looked after me post-surgery. I decided they deserved two boxes of chocolates, but shh, don't tell the ward that!

I didn't want to just drop off the chocolates to them; I wanted them to see me leave, to see me walking out, moving forward, proving that their care had worked.

The smiles on their faces when I handed over the card and treats were priceless. It wasn't just thanks - it was closure, for all of us.

Not everything was smooth, of course. Some staples still needed to come out, which I understood. A new nurse came by, a burly bloke, full of wit and charm. He removed half the staples and said the rest would need to come out next week. He went off to arrange for a district nurse to come to my house on Monday. Well, that didn't go to plan! He came back in a huff, explaining how the district nurse refused, saying *"if he can walk, he doesn't need me to come round"*. He shouted at her and slammed down the phone! He apologised to me; he had tried to have my best interests at heart. Even on my last day, the chaos of hospital life didn't let up.

Packing my bag didn't take long at all and by then, my Mom had arrived to wait with me.

Now, it was time to go through the release form. The nurse read it out loud to me, it sounded like some sort of contract, however, no matter what it said, I wanted to get out of there today, so let's get it signed!

A few more checks to do and ticked off the list. Next, time for my prescription. Opioids block your system, so no morphine or oramorph; paracetamol was the only thing offered. I was a little shocked, would I be able to cope and manage my pain at home? Let's not worry, let's focus on positives - you're going home TODAY!

One of the nurses from EPOC came to see me on the ward as she wasn't there when I handed over the card and chocolates. She gave me a hug and said good luck. One last thing though:

"This is where the hard part starts".

I took the advice in my stride and with a smile, but boy, would she be right!

One of my oldest mates Jon came to pick me up, what a legend. He'd taken the day off work and just said to let him know when I was ready. A huge gesture in my mind that meant so much to me. That's what 30 years of friendship truly means.

It was time to leave. We headed downstairs; I'm not sure what emotion I felt as we were going. The anger and frustration of the ward had clouded me; I was frustrated and more annoyed than anything else but I knew I didn't want these emotions to be at the top of my agenda. I was headed home, this was amazing, it was progress. The hospital doors automatically opened and I was hit with fresh air for the first time in 10 days. Out into the car park, concrete under my feet, it felt good!

I saw Jon's car and in we got. He drove incredibly carefully, making sure that any bumps wouldn't affect me. The journey wasn't too long and I said my thanks to him. Another manly hug given. **I was home**. Up a few steps and key in the door.

Home at Last

It felt fantastic to be home. 10 long days in hospital had drained me to my very core - my body, my mind, my soul.

To step through my own front door again was liberating. I'd missed my house, it's creaks, it's cracks, it's quirks. To see my home comforts, my own walls, my plants and some colour at last! I'd remembered the smell of my vanilla and oud diffuser, this was my place, my house, my home. There's something so comforting in just saying "I'm home".

First things first, a brew!! Knowing me I probably wanted to make it myself, but knowing my Mom, I'm sure there was no way she would've let me! So, sit down, rest, take it slow.

The cuppa comes. Hold on, what's this? A brand-new mug to say welcome home...in leopard print! It immediately brought a smile to my face; my Mom knows me so well! This was more than simply a mug, it symbolised who I was and it was a gift to celebrate being back after everything I'd been through.

My mom would stay with me for 5 weeks; there's no way I could've coped lived alone. Rest, rest and more rest; I had found it almost impossible to rest in hospital. The constant beeping of machines, the blood tests, temperature checks, the bloke next to me snoring like he was a bear, it was horrendous. At home, I had my comforts. I could go upstairs and just lie down, in my own bed. Safely knowing my Mom was only a text away. We joked saying I'd need a bell like the guy off breaking bad, a tea bell I called it! Didn't happen, shame, I still want that tea bell! Ding!

The first night wasn't easy - my night sweats and restless legs continued. My Mom was in the spare room next door and I text her at midnight to help me. I was drenched. I was unable to change the sheets, unable to bend down. The scar was tight, my body sore. I felt useless. But this is what my Mom was there for, to help me, to care for me, to look after me. What a superstar.

2am came. Drenched again, so I messaged my Mom. She opened the door within minutes and I apologised and felt a sense of embarrassment. She hugged me and said *"it's all OK. Let's change these sheets and get them in the wash"*. Fresh sheets let's try to sleep and relax as best I can, I was wiped out.

3am - it's happened again, cold and soaking wet sheets. Not just a little sweat, the sheets were drenched through, it was horrible. I lay there for a little bit, not wanting to constantly wake my Mom up. However, it was no burden, *I* was no burden, so she came to my rescue again, clearly very tired, but more than happy to help and keep me sane.

The night sweats continued every night for ten days, you can image the toll and strain that put on both of us. But, if there's one thing I've learnt from my Mom, it's that you can carry on, look after the people that love you and nothing is too hard to accomplish.

There was a lot to think about. I had daily injections to do, an anti-coagulant. This wasn't a pleasant start to the day; to inject myself, it was a shot to the stomach or thigh. I never quite grasped the technique. Prod at an angle and press in. Different spot each day, when it's done, pop the needle in a sharps bin that was provided. The injections left horrible and painful bruises all over my already bruised stomach. Now I know how a pin cushion feels!

I couldn't just sit still, but I couldn't go far either. I needed a happy medium. My toilet was upstairs, so at least I could go up and down for my exercise and do some sort of physiotherapy at home. My mom would always worry, sometimes waiting at the bottom of the stairs *"just in case"*. My usual response would be "you may as well do us a new brew now then".

I absolutely loved having my Mom live with me. I was more quiet than usual and didn't have the energy to binge watch series or do much at all. We usually have deep chats about anything and everything, but I just couldn't manage conversations at times and sometimes I'd just sit there in silence with my eyes closed. That's ok, my Mom had her puzzle book to keep her busy! It was a comfort to know she was there next to me.

Monday - time for the rest of my staples to come out. As the district nurse refused to come to my house (I mean, come on, I'd just had a major cancer operation), I walked slowly and carefully to the doctors. It's not far, but it was my Everest that day. Take it easy, you're ok.

I'd been given the little snipping tool to remove the staples and handed this to the nurse. By now, more scabs had formed, almost healing over the staples - me thinks this won't be as easy as once thought!

Snip! Ping! Ouch! 27 staples to come out of the most tender part of me, grimacing with each one, a sharp pain, a nick here, a tightness there. Some needed a little more oomph as they had scabbed over. Some weren't as bad. But all done within 15 mins, phew. Another thing off the list!

The next morning, I woke up with what can only be described as a leaky belly. That's right, part of my scar seemed OPEN. I didn't panic, I don't think I had that feeling in me anymore. Once you go through major surgery, you kinda just shrug these things off and say, oh well, better get this sorted. I pressed near the hole. It made a hissing sound and more fluid came out, not bloody, but not exactly clear. Time to ring the hospital!

Apparently, it was "only" inflammatory fluid, and I was told to go back to my GP and get them to sort it. An emergency appointment is quite easy to get when you say that you've just had your staples removed after a cancer op and now your stomach is leaking!

I got a taxi to the doctors this time, I didn't exactly fancy a walk with fluid dripping down me. The GP and nurse checked it out and agreed nothing looked like an infection. They put on two saline patches and some gauze and told me to keep it covered for a few days. *"Keep an eye on it and if anything changes, call the hospital immediately"*.

I was honestly fine, calm in fact, I probably even found it quite amusing in a way and no doubt made a sarcastic comment to the nurse and doctor.

I've survived my whole life with sarcasm. With bad puns and silly jokes, the worse, the better. When everything feels out of your control, there's power in laughing at the madness. I'd made dark comments because humour was my armour. It doesn't mean you're not scared - it just means that you've found a way to function without falling apart.

After a few days, I took the gauze off to let it air, all seemed fine. Phew, relief! Over the next few days, the scar changed. Without the staples it widened and widened. It was actually quite fascinating to see; I could see the healing process happening day by day. Not saying that I wasn't in pain or discomfort, but it did give me hope as already I saw a physical change in my body.

The first few weeks stayed like that, a routine almost. This was recovery. It needed to be slow and calm. My Mom helped me with everything; cleaning, washing up, cups of tea when I needed one and of course, my food.

I needed a nap every single day. I'd go upstairs to bed for rest, slowly and carefully, there was no way I'd risk anything. My Mom would always say, *"text me if you need anything"*. It was a huge comfort knowing she was there for me. I've always been hugely independent and stubborn with it most times; I want things done my way, it's my house and I'll do it! But time for being, stubborn was over. I needed help, I needed care and I needed my Mom's love to look after me.

The Cancer Free Call

A month had passed since my operation; it was time for my biopsy results and nerves were extremely high. This is what I wanted, wasn't it? To be told I was cancer free. That was the goal of all of this after all - to survive.

I knew the call was coming from Mr Shariff. We had agreed on a phone call instead of me driving an hour to the hospital, meeting him, then driving an hour back.

I was anxious. My Mom was still taking care of me. The phone rang and I put it on loudspeaker. I heard the words *"cancer free"* and *"successful operation"*. I can't remember much else. My mind went blank. I'm not sure where I drifted to, it's all a blur. I was quiet, not really responsive. I didn't know what to say. It felt like an anti-climax and I was confused. Was this real? I was still recovering, my stomach was still covered in scabs and I was still in pain. There wasn't a joyous moment, no rush of emotion, no endorphins, I just felt flat and numb. I couldn't process it. It wasn't like TV or films; I wasn't ringing a bell or high fiving anyone. I was sitting on my sofa. It felt distant, even though this was what I wanted and what I needed to hear – "cancer free".

The reality of what I'd been through suddenly hit me. I'd really had cancer and I'd gone through a life-changing operation. Half my body had been opened up; I'd had the most aggressive surgery possible and the scar would be with me for life. I had been in fight mode for so long and suddenly it was gone. The ceiling had been lifted and I was left staring at the empty space above me. Now what? What am I fighting for? Who am I? What do I do?

The truth is that the call didn't bring closure. It hit me hard, I couldn't process the moment, I realised I had changed forever. I felt lost. I didn't know what would happen next. Am I really cancer free? Will it come back?

What I've learned since then is that "cancer free" is not just about what the doctors say, It's not only about scans or test results, but also about the slow process of reclaiming life. At first, I thought I had to feel joy straight away, that I had to be instantly grateful and full of energy. But life doesn't work like that. Healing takes time and sometimes good news needs space to sink in.

Being told I was cancer free didn't mean everything was instantly easy. It meant I had been given another chance. At first, that felt overwhelming. What do I do with this chance? How do I live differently? But over time I realised I don't need to do something extraordinary to deserve survival. Living itself is extraordinary. Cooking dinner, laughing with my Mom, watching birds in the garden, hearing music I love - these things matter more than I ever knew before.

I also learned that being cancer free doesn't mean being free of fear. The "what if" question still lingers in the back of my mind. But instead of letting it paralyse me, I try to use it as a reminder. A reminder to value the day I'm in, to focus on what I can control and to stop putting things off.

One day I was standing in front of the mirror, looking at my scar. Instead of seeing it as something ugly, I tried to see it differently. It's proof I came through, It's a mark of survival, a reminder of what I was strong enough to endure and that my body is still carrying me forward. That shift in perspective didn't happen overnight, but when it did, it helped me breathe easier.

Over time the numbness of that phone call softened and I started to let in gratitude. Gratitude that I got to hear those words at all, gratitude that I was given time that I might not have had, gratitude for the people who carried me through my darkest moments. And slowly I began to understand that the flatness I felt wasn't failure, It wasn't me "wasting" the moment, It was simply shock. Survival doesn't always come with fireworks. Sometimes it comes quietly, in a living room, through a speakerphone. And maybe that's alright. What matters is what comes next. I didn't dance around the room when I heard the words, but I can dance later. I didn't cry tears of joy on the sofa, but I can shed them when I watch a sunset, or when I realise I've gone a whole day without thinking about cancer. The moment doesn't have to be cinematic to be meaningful.

So yes, the call felt strange and it left me numb, but it also gave me the chance to move forward, to rediscover myself, to live in a way that honours what I've been through. Cancer free is not the end of the story. It's the start of a new one.

If you're reading this and you're waiting for your own call, or if you've had it and felt underwhelmed like I did, know this: it's ok; You don't have to feel how films tell you to feel, you don't have to be a poster child for survival, you just have to be you.

The day I was told I was cancer free wasn't the happiest day of my life. But it was the day that gave me the rest of my life. And that's something worth celebrating, every single day I wake up.

Life's an Adventure

Life's an adventure, a journey untold.
With eyes open wide, I venture into the bold.
The pages are blank, the ink yet to spill, I shape the story,
I guide my own will.
The path is uncertain, yet filled with grace,
I step into the unknown, no need to erase.
Like a pirate, I sail towards the dawn,
with love in my heart and courage reborn.
I'll learn from the winds and grow with each tide,
embrace every moment and stand there with pride.
With a cup of tea in my hand, I'm able to breathe,
grateful for the moments I'm yet to achieve.
Last year wasn't the end, just a twist in the plot,
my story's still going and it's far from forgot.

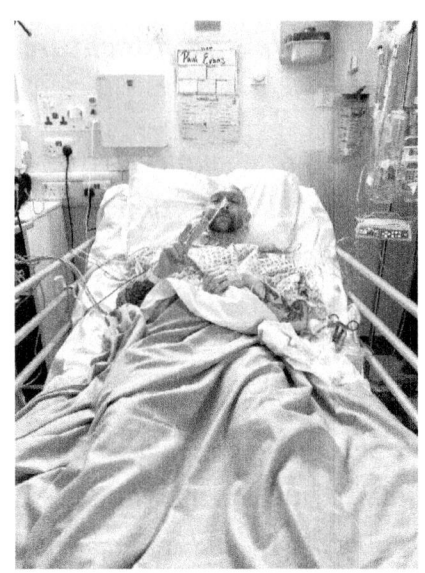

Straight after my op.

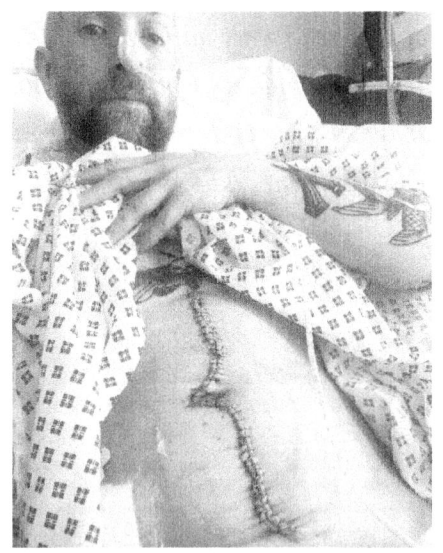

First time seeing my scar.

Always there for me.

My mom's 75th.

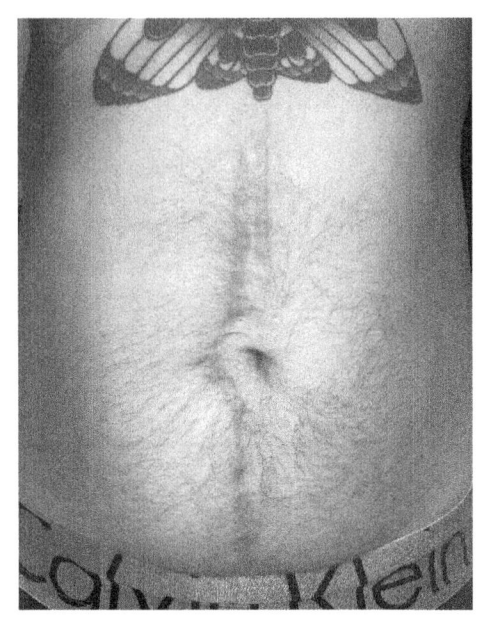

Healing well – a year on.

Art Market.

This tattoo meant so much to me; a visual reminder of who I am and what I've been through.

Time For a Brew

I boil the water, I steep the leaves,
the anxiety halters, that's what this achieves.
The process continues, the mind goes free,
in 5 minutes, time, it's time for tea!
A mindful act, it's simple, yet true with he-man's face,
it's the perfect brew!
With Barry's in my hand, I take the first sip,
there's no need for biscuits, I'll never dip!
The act is complete, now I'm warm and calm,
ready to face the day and embrace all its charm.

Professor Beggs: the Man, the Myth, the Legend

I received a letter saying that my cancer care would now be under another consultant, Prof Beggs, Professor of Cancer Genetics & Surgery and Deputy Director of the Birmingham Experimental Cancer Medicine Centre.

My first appointment with him was for September. I got to the hospital early; I had decided to go on my own this time. I sat down, my name was called and I was greeted with a handshake and a beaming smile; a beast of a man (I mean, I'm 5'5"!) and we went into his office where a student would also be present.

Firstly, he asked how I was. Wow, I didn't think that would make me so emotional, but it did, someone actually wanted to know how I was first, and he genuinely meant it. I was seen; I was being heard. I told him I was struggling with my mental health, but that I'd reached out to Birmingham Healthy Minds. He said those are the people he would've recommended, this was going well I thought to myself! He wanted to know how my recovery was going, so we continued talking; it felt very calm and nice to talk to a professional who clearly cared and wanted to know how I was doing.

Now, down to business. A little look over my notes, my symptoms and what had happened previously. He told me why he had taken over my care and that he was truly sorry with what happened at the start with my appendix and then how I was diagnosed. This shouldn't have been the way.

He told me what would happen next under his care. Then, the serious side. Let's talk about what he does as a research professor and why I'm there.

There's something called Lynch Syndrome (I'll dive into this in more detail in the next chapter). Firstly, let's do a family tree to discuss cancer and genetics, let's look at who has been affected if you know and find out what we can learn. "

You'll need your genetics tested and you'll need some other blood tests as well. Now, let's discuss your complex polypectomy you had a week before your operation in May. They removed 9 polyps, when is your next one?"

Well, I was actually hoping it would be next year, I'd had two major operations this year and thought my body could do with the rest.

"Ideally, I'd like you to get it done sooner".

Ok, I completely understood that tone and what it meant! Scans, cameras and colonoscopies were vital to protect and detect anything nasty, so I told him that as soon as I got home, I'd book one.

We then discussed why; The possibility of me having Serrated Polyposis Syndrome, what this was and what it meant, the potential that these were pre-cancerous in my bowel.

3 months after I was given the cancer free call, I'm told in less than half an hour about the potential of two other cancers. I was in shock and the fear kicked in again. It wasn't over, not by a long shot.

Lynch Syndrome

Hearing that I potentially had Lynch Syndrome was gut wrenching. I felt sick, anxious, and the initial trauma of being diagnosed with cancer was back. The doubts, the fears, the "it's not over" was in full force. I was scared.

When you get diagnosed with cancer, suddenly a whole new dictionary lands in your lap. You start hearing words and phrases you've never heard before, or you've heard them but never wanted to know too much about them. One of those phrases for me was 'Lynch Syndrome'. It's an inherited genetic condition that increases your risk of developing certain types of cancer - most commonly bowel (colorectal) cancer, but also stomach, ovarian, womb and others. Basically, if you have it, your body's natural ability to repair DNA damage isn't working as it should and that means that rogue cells can slip through the cracks and grow into tumours far more easily. It's caused by a mutation in one of a handful of genes responsible for DNA repair - think of them like your body's proofreaders. Normally, these proofreaders spot mistakes when your cells are copying themselves and fix them before they cause trouble. With Lynch Syndrome however, one of the proofreaders is missing or asleep on the job, and those mistakes can turn into cancer.

It's not exactly rare - it's estimated that around 1 in every 300 people might have it - but the awareness of it is shockingly low. Many people don't even know it exists until it turns up in their medical notes or in those of a family member and because Lynch Syndrome is hereditary, it can pass down through generations. That's one of the reasons it's so important - if one person is diagnosed, it's not just about their health, it's about their children, their siblings, and even extended family. Knowing you have Lynch Syndrome can mean earlier screening and regular checks that can literally save lives.

For those who do test positive, life changes. You'll likely be monitored closely, with colonoscopies every year or two, and screening for other cancers depending on your age, sex and family history. It's not exactly anyone's idea of fun, but the flip side is that it massively increases the chances of catching cancer early, when it's most treatable. And while the science is important, it's the human side of it that's harder to digest. Imagine knowing that your DNA - the very code that makes you - is carrying a built-in fault. Imagine knowing that your children have a 50% chance of inheriting that same fault. That's a heavy weight to carry.

When my doctors first brought it up, I felt like my head was already overflowing with enough acronyms, statistics and horror stories and I didn't want another one to add to the list, but I also understood why it mattered. If I had Lynch Syndrome, it could explain part of why I got cancer and it would mean my niece and nephews might be at higher risk too. It wasn't just about me anymore, so, I went through the process: Genetic counselling, the blood test, the waiting. The waiting is its own kind of torture, you start thinking about every relative who's had cancer, every story you've heard, every "what if".

Then the results came in – negative! I don't have Lynch Syndrome. I can't tell you the relief I felt. Not just for me, but for my family; my niece and nephews would've needed testing and how do you tell them that? It didn't take away the cancer I'd already had, but it took away the thought that I might have one day pass down something dangerous.

I'm still glad I went through the testing though. Knowledge is power, even if it's not the news you want. And if you're reading this and have a family history of certain cancers, it's worth asking the question. Because Lynch Syndrome isn't just a line in a medical journal - it's real, it's here, and for some people, catching it early can make all the difference.

Lynch Syndrome — At a glance

- **What it is**: An inherited genetic condition that increases the risk of several cancers, especially bowel, womb, ovarian, and stomach.
- **Cause**: Mutation in one of the genes responsible for repairing DNA damage.
- **How common**: Around 1 in every 300 people may have it - most don't know.
- **Inheritance**: If a parent has it, there's a 50% chance their child will too.
- **Management**: Regular screening such as colonoscopies and other cancer checks, starting earlier than the general population.
- **Why it matters**: Early detection saves lives. Testing can protect not just you, but your family.

Serrated Polyposis Syndrome

When you hear the word 'cancer,' you expect certain things - surgery, chemo, scans. But no one warned me about something called **Serrated Polyposis Syndrome**, or SPS. I quickly learnt that it would become a big part of my story and my life.

So, what is SPS? Well, it means having a large number of serrated polyps in your bowel. Polyps are little growths that form on the lining of your bowel. Most people might get a small polyp or two now and then - not unusual. But with SPS, there are lots, sometimes dozens and these polyps are not your usual mushroom shaped kind - they're flat and sharp, they can hide in the folds of your bowel, which makes them particularly tricky to spot.

In simple terms, SPS is a rare condition that means you're prone to developing multiple serrated polyps in your colon and rectum. Polyps are essentially growths in the lining of your bowel, and serrated ones are shaped a bit like saw blades under a microscope - hence the name.

While not every polyp will turn cancerous, SPS carries a significantly increased risk of bowel cancer. That's why, once you've been diagnosed, your life gets a lot more about scopes, screenings, and awkward hospital gowns than you ever imagined. It's not glamorous and there are no "miracle diets" to make it vanish. It's a lifelong condition, and it means my relationship with the NHS endoscopy team is now closer than most of my friendships.

This was a bit of a shock to me. Imagine the doctors telling you: "*You've got around 40 polyps in your bowel*". I'd only just recently had bowel surgery, with 30% of it taken out!

This meant multiple colonoscopies and procedures called polypectomies, where they snip and snare out the polyps one by one. Not exactly my idea of a fun day out, but absolutely necessary.

I soon learned these polyps can be sneaky - they sometimes lurk in places a normal camera can miss. That's why the medical team use special techniques during the procedure - spraying a purple dye and inflating the bowel with water and air to make sure nothing was hiding. It's unpleasant, you feel bloated and have discomfort, but the alternative is far worse.

I always opt for sedation, you're awake, but you are definitely more comfortable; Gas and air too if it's available! Stay still and try to relax, it's not nice, but it needs doing.

The camera has a little loop or snare on the end; this wraps itself around the polyps and takes them out - clever stuff! They move you as gently as they can and they manoeuvre the camera around your bowel as easily as they can (you have about 9 meters, all wrapped up, so it's tricky!). You get your report straight after, showing you what they've done and what they've taken out.

A Few Things to Know About SPS

- SPS is quite rare, so you might not have heard of it before, and you might feel a bit isolated when you get this diagnosis.

- It does increase your risk of bowel cancer, which is why regular checks are vital.

- Removal of these polyps can prevent them from turning into cancer, which is why those colonoscopies are so important.

- The exact cause isn't fully understood, but genetics seem to play a role - but it's nobody's fault.

- It's not about lifestyle or diet; you didn't bring this on yourself.

My Experience

Having all these procedures is tough, physically and mentally. The bowel prep alone is something I dread even now. Drinking that awful salt solution feels like punishment, but it's absolutely necessary.

The colonoscopy itself is uncomfortable, to say the least. Watching the screen while the camera explores places you'd rather forget isn't something everyone wants to do, but for me, knowing what's going on helped me feel more in control. I speak to the technician and ask them questions during my procedure; this focussed my mind.

On top of that, finding out about SPS meant I needed more frequent check-ups, which means more hospital visits and more time spent wondering what they might find next.

Advice for Anyone Facing SPS

- Don't skip your screenings - they really are lifesaving.
- If you don't understand something, ask. It's your body and your health.
- Don't be afraid to lean on your support network - you don't have to go through it alone.
- Find little things that bring you peace and focus on them - for me, it's my drawing and nature.
- Remember, while SPS increases risks, it doesn't mean cancer is inevitable. Catching and removing polyps early is a huge win.

SPS might not be something that you expect on your cancer journey, but it's a reminder that health isn't always straightforward. It's a bit like life - full of twists and surprises. But with the right care and attitude, you can handle it.

SPS added another layer of anxiety to an already tough year; You don't just deal with the physical discomfort but also the mental toll. Waiting for results, worrying if new polyps have appeared, wondering if one might have turned cancerous - it's a lot. That's where talking helped me. Whether it was with my Mom, Millsy, my therapist, my TikTok friends, I found sharing my fears made them feel less monstrous. And distraction became my friend; Drawing, walking in nature, focusing on the little joys helped pull me back from the edge on tough days.

And through it all, I'm determined to live fully - to embrace joy, laughter, and even the sarcastic humour that saved me when things felt darkest.

Let's Talk About the Diving Board

There's this thing I always say about anxiety - it's like a diving board, the climb up is the worst part and every step, you feel it. Nerves. Doubt. Panic. "What if I slip?" "What if it hurts?" "What if I can't do it?" But the moment you actually jump off - that's the part that's over in seconds. It's freeing, it's the fun part.

The lesson? The climb - the overthinking, the dread, the build-up - is almost always worse than the actual event. Waiting for test results, waiting for appointments, waiting for life to make sense again... it's all diving board. It's hell but it's also a huge part of having cancer. Sometimes you have to ignore the what ifs; Yes, the anxiety builds up, but sometimes you have to just DO IT.

Fatigue: Batteries Not Included

Well, this isn't a fun part at all. Brian fog, headaches, confusion, dizziness, low mood, energy zapped and drained, wanting to stay in bed, no motivation. Fatigue has stopped me wanting to meet up with people, go places, do things. It's created its own anxiety, its own way of life, some days it wins, others I say, "not a chance". It has its own force and some sort of control over me.

If you've ever experienced it, you'll know that it feels like your power source is low and you need recharging, or better still, some new batteries!

Your body can feel heavy, your thoughts sluggish, and even the smallest task can seem like climbing a hill in wellies filled with cement (not that I've tried that). It can hit without warning too; one day you might feel almost normal, the next you're floored. It doesn't care if you have plans, people to see or tasks to do. I've felt absolutely fine one hour and then suddenly, bam, it hits me.

Fatigue can mess with your concentration and your memory too. You forget words mid-sentence, lose your train of thought, or stare at a cupboard wondering why you opened it. I probably came into the kitchen for a brew, so may as well have one! It's frustrating, invisible to most people and hard to explain without sounding lazy or dramatic.

People will tell you to "just rest" or "have a nap" as if it's a magic cure. What they don't get is that rest doesn't always help, sometimes you wake up just as exhausted as when you lay down. It's like the fatigue is part of you now, etched into your skin.

There's also the mental side of it. You can feel too tired to focus, too tired to hold a conversation, too tired to even choose what to watch on TV. Before my cancer operation I'd happily binge, a TV series and find so much enjoyment in it. Now, I really struggle. You start to ration your energy like it's a precious currency. If I go out for lunch, that's the day gone. If I meet someone for coffee, I probably can't cook dinner later, so it'll be cereals.

One of the hardest bits is explaining it to people. You can't see fatigue, there's no plaster or bandage, so people think you're fine because *"you look fine"*.

It's not all doom and gloom though - Fatigue has taught me to prioritise myself for once. I've learnt to say no without guilt, to stop over-committing and to save my energy for what actually matters.

What helps?

Listen to your body. Sometimes you honestly need a day in bed. Sometimes, you have to fight against it. You have survived cancer; you need to live! Go the gym, get fresh air, see friends, yes, the fatigue is there but it'll be worth it! Do what you can and what you feel will give you the best result. Some days you can't do much, others you can push through and get out there.

Fatigue is still one of the most frustrating leftovers from cancer - a constant reminder that even though the big battles might be over, the war leaves scars that you can't always see.

Fatigue - At a Glance

- Common after cancer and its treatments - affects up to 90% of patients at some stage.
- Can be physical, mental or both.
- Rest and sleep don't always improve it.
- Often unpredictable - good days and bad days come with no warning.
- Can last months or even years after treatment ends.
- Impacts memory, focus and decision making.
- Energy needs to be "budgeted" carefully to avoid crashes.
- It is invisible to others, which can make it hard to explain or for people to understand.

Interpersonal Psychotherapy (IPP): Yikes That Sounds Scary!

I knew I was struggling; The trauma my body and mind had been through had finally taken its toll and I knew I needed professional help. I reached out to Birmingham Healthy Minds; I was assessed and told the best course of action would be a form of trauma therapy, IPP, but there was a 4-month waiting list. That's fine, at least I was on the list, at least I've made that first contact and knowing there would be help soon had brought me some comfort.

My mental health declined, I'd beaten cancer; there was NO WAY depression was gonna beat me. I bought a journal as I wanted to take this seriously. The journal needed to be visually striking, I needed that stimulus to make me use it. Before my sessions started, I wrote down some thoughts; They were negative and they filled an entire page, just words. I knew this wasn't good, so the next day, I started a positives list, yes, this also filled the page, progress!

When my therapy started, we chatted about anything I wanted. My therapist explained it would take 4 months for the sessions, once a week. She outlined a plan of action, homework, ways of thinking etc.

I honestly don't remember my childhood. It's blank, there's bits here and there, like my Mom always making a special b'day cake for me, but apart from that, it wasn't an enjoyable upbringing. I was shy, quiet and only had love from one parent, but it turns out, that's all I needed.

I knew I didn't want to open Pandora's box, I'm in trauma therapy, let's not add anymore!

I wanted progress and to move on, to have coping mechanisms when my depression kicked in and my therapist agreed, let's focus on what I've just been through, then the now and then the future.

My sessions would be every Thursday via a phone call. I'd just had a knee op (yes, during my recovery!) but, having the calls was way better, I could get comfy, have my trusty cuppa and try to be more relaxed at home, plus, I had no excuses not to take the call.

The first five sessions were incredibly tough. I needed my bed straight after, I was drained. It would take nearly until the next session to gain my energy back.

I learnt that I'd never loved myself and I'd always doubted myself. I'd go out and always believed I would be physically or verbally attacked. If I saw someone walking towards me, what were they gonna say?! I needed to build an answer in my head and be prepared, anxiety grew, anger grew, but as always, they simply walked past and continued with their day. The next person walking, they are laughing, is it me? Is it what I'm wearing? The self-doubt and constant self-put me downs had been there for an incredibly long time. I had developed a learnt version of myself, but it wasn't real. My anxiety would grow, it made me think everyone and everything was against me, and I lived in fear.

I portrayed confidence, fun, sarcastic, silly, sometimes annoying, but it was a mask. I was hiding, faking it until you make it. I was struggling and had been all my life. I felt like a failure in everything; I'm single, I'm a freelancer, I'm tired, I'm ill. The list could and did go on and on and on. I'd get headaches and feel sick to my stomach, I'd avoid seeing people, doing things. If I did, I'd cope by drinking way too much, to forget what was going on in my head, to stop the noise.

I could wear my leopard print shirt and my best aftershave like armour, but I'd still have that self-doubt. What if someone says something? It would immediately knock my confidence and I'd internally crumble and become a shell of myself.

The IPP sessions continued, I'd write notes in my journal every time, not knowing if I'd ever revisit them, but knowing it helped to jot things down. I knew this was the process; I wanted to talk, to listen and to make small notes. My therapist gave me little tasks along the way, *"think of this for next week, think about the 'whys', the 'whens' and the physical aspects that connect to the mental"*.

After the 5th session, things changed, *I* changed. We started chatting more positively and we looked at how and why I feel the way I do, the fact that I had contradicting emotions and feelings. I have huge empathy and want to help others, yet I can't help myself! If I removed myself for a moment and looked from a distance, I'd want to help that person and feel sorry for them, yet, put myself back in my body and I found that difficult, that was a huge revelation. Why can't I help myself? It's not selfish at all! She helped me realise so many things; the way I think or react in situations, she taught me to accept my feelings and emotions. Therapy really has changed my life for the better. I'm a completely different person now. I perceive life differently and look at myself differently. It's so empowering.

My therapist was truly amazing and I cannot thank her enough. She gave me so much hope and belief, she always championed me and said how well I was doing. For the first time in my life I can truly say I love myself and I'm proud of who I am. One session she said:

"Art is a gift you've been given, embrace it".

What a truly wonderful thing to have said to you. She taught me that art is beautiful, *MY* art is beautiful, I'm allowed to look and it and think "wow".

Therapy also reminded me that I can't help everyone. I like listening to people's problems, I like giving advice from my experience. People have shared so much with me but not every problem is mine to solve; I can give my advice, my thoughts, my ideas, but if they don't take them, then that's ok! I can only give so much.

The sessions were invaluable. I still have depression and anxiety, I don't think that will ever leave me, but I'm able to look at things differently now, to not worry as much, to understand that I can and will get through this. I have worth and value and I deserve to acknowledge that.

Drawing My Way Back

When you go through cancer, you lose so much more than your health. You lose your sense of safety. You lose parts of your identity. And for me, somewhere in the chaos of appointments and treatments, I lost my quiet. The world felt loud, my head even louder.

I didn't plan to start drawing again. I used to draw loads when I was really young, then in my teenage years I'd doodle all over my schoolbooks with gremlins and trolls. Then, I simply stopped.

I'd bought a journal ready for my therapy and jotted down some notes, then I did a doodle and showed this on TikTok, and my good friend Mel said I should carry on. Nah, they're just doodles I thought! Then she bought me a sketch book and pencils and this opened up my world!

I started off with just 5-minute pencil sketches of animals. I'm a perfectionist, so even though these were only 5 minutes drawings, it still caused me stress and I wanted them to be better!

One day I took an hour to draw - wow, this changed everything! I was calmer, felt at ease, took my time to shade and add shadows and it looked really good!

I can share what I've done and find joy in my own work, I can look at it and think, "hold on, YOU did that". It's also brought me closer to my Mom, she loves her crafts and through art, we connected even more which I didn't think was possible!

It's more than just drawing. It's given me a purpose, a focus, it helps quieten the noise, it's a passion and a hobby. It makes me feel proud and finally believe in myself. I can take a literal blank canvas and express myself and be creative.

For the first time in months, I was somewhere else in my head. Not in a hospital ward, not in a waiting room, but in that quiet space you get when you're fully focused on something you love.

Drawing set up: It's important to get your surroundings right. A tranquil, quiet place away from the normality of life and noise. My dining room is the perfect place for me; I have a large table, almost like a Vikings dinner table! I have my plants (that reminds me, I must water them) and my crystals (lapis lazuli, various quartz, labradorite and some agates to name a few). It has a huge window letting in loads of light which leads out to my garden where I can hear and see the birds. It allows me to be in the moment yet also have mindfulness. It's quiet, away from the road (living in a city can be pretty noisy)!

I grab myself a cuppa, sit down, open the sketch book on a fresh page and begin. Even saying that, 'a fresh page' has its own meaning, drawing is so symbolic. I have an idea of what I'll draw and then the blank canvas becomes its own thing; I can use my methodical mind to resolve any problems that may occur. The "little mistakes" are now part of the process, they're enjoyable and I embrace them. That's the beauty of art therapy, it's not about creating a masterpiece, it's about creating space. A mental breather, a safe place where the only thing that matters is the line you're drawing, the colour you're blending, the shape slowly appearing on the page. The canvas was blank and now suddenly, it isn't.

There's a lot of science behind it; When you're absorbed in making art, your brain shifts into a calmer state; Stress hormones drop, your breathing slows. It's mindfulness in disguise and unlike meditation, where you might sit there wondering if you're doing it right, drawing gives you something to hold, something to see.

For cancer recovery, this is powerful. Treatment can make you feel like your body isn't yours anymore. Art hands some of that control back as you get to decide what goes on the page, you set the pace and you choose the colours, the strokes, the subject. And that choice - however small - matters.

For me, drawing animals became my thing. Tigers, leopards, chameleons - sometimes realistic, sometimes not. It didn't matter if they were perfect, what mattered was the peace I felt while creating them and the pride I felt when they were done. Each drawing became a quiet reminder: *you can still make beautiful things.* I learned finally that it didn't matter if I "failed", the odd bit of smudge here, gone over the lines there, it was part of the process and it was fun!

Art therapy doesn't have to be formal. You don't need classes or expensive materials, just a pencil and scrap of paper will do. Some people find joy in painting, others in collage, some in clay or textiles. The medium doesn't matter - it's the process that heals. And here's the thing: the benefits aren't just psychological. Creative activity can help with physical recovery too; Fine motor skills improve, your focus sharpens, you become more aware of your body in a gentle, positive way.

I've also found that art is a way of talking about things without having to actually talk. You can pour emotions into colour and shape; you can tell your story without having to find the right words. Sometimes, I've looked back at something I've drawn and realised it was saying something I hadn't yet admitted out loud.

I saw a local competition online, calling for artist to showcase their work with the winners becoming part of an art trail. I thought 'why not?' Let's enter and forget about it. So, I chose my best drawings, both vibrant and colourful - a kingfisher and a peacock. To my surprise, two weeks later at around 11pm, I received an email: "Congratulations - You've been selected!" Wow, my art had been chosen! I was so chuffed! Full of pride and glee, I immediately messaged my Mom!

The artwork was displayed in a children's book shop, on show for all the world to see (well, at least a small part of it)! It gave me a huge sense of achievement; I'd only been drawing for about 5 months and people in the art community had seen my work and celebrated it. It was a huge confidence boost that I needed. A boost that would push my artwork further; I could achieve, I could so more.

It also meant that I received a lot of complements, prompting another new and exciting venture that I never expected to do, a craft fair! I was nervous, excited and curious to see what would happen. It was invigorating to showcase my drawings and see how people reacted to it.

For anyone recovering from cancer, art can be both a distraction and a bridge back to yourself. It's time spent creating instead of worrying. It's proof that you're more than a diagnosis. And maybe that's the most healing thing of all.

These Boots Are Made For Walking

Walking sounds almost too simple to make a difference, yet it can be one of the most powerful tools during cancer recovery. No gym membership, no expensive kit, just you, a pair of comfy trainers and somewhere to go. It also brought me back to a time before cancer, where I used to walk along the canals in Birmingham. Have I mentioned that Birmingham has more canals than Venice?

Physically, it gets your heart working, strengthens muscles and keeps joints moving. It helps circulation, lowers the risk of blood clots and can even improve digestion. For many people, it's a gentle way to rebuild stamina after surgery or treatment without pushing the body too far. It can also help keep weight stable, which in turn supports recovery and overall health.

The benefits aren't just physical - many find that a short walk is the perfect way to process thoughts, calm nerves and regain a sense of control. I find it gives me a sense of freedom like nothing else.

Psychologically, walking can clear your head. Fresh air, a change of scenery, the steady rhythm of your footsteps - it's a quiet reminder that you're still moving forward. It can lift mood, ease anxiety and help you sleep better. Some days it's about distance, others it's just about getting out the front door. Both count.

For cancer survivors, walking can feel like reclaiming something that illness tried to take away. It's proof that your body still works; that you can move, that you can choose where to go next. It can help reduce cancer-related fatigue, improve immune function and even lower the risk of recurrence in some cancers.

Walking outdoors adds another layer to it; You notice the seasons change, the sound of birds, the smell after rain. You also start to notice small things - the colour of a leaf, a crack in the pavement, a neighbour's cat that always seems to be watching you. These moments pull you into the present, away from worry about test results or hospital letters. Nature has a way of quietly reminding you that life keeps moving, no matter what.

It's not about speed or counting steps (unless you want to). It's about finding a pace that suits you and making it part of your routine. Some walks will be slow and short; some will be longer - The important part is that you're doing it. Walking reminds you that your body that - even after everything it's been through - it can still carry you forward. It's literally one step at a time and that really does add up.

Positivity, positivity, positivity: On one of my walks, I suddenly had an epiphany; I'd had a text from someone asking me how I was. My usual response was ALWAYS "erm, not bad". However, today I was way better than just not too bad, I was feeling pretty damn good in fact! For one of the first times in my life, I accepted and acknowledged that! I realised this was part of my negative mindset and one day, I just changed it, like a toggle had been flipped in my brain. I answer more realistically now, if I'm in a good place I respond, "I'm really good thanks, how are you?" accepting and embracing it. If I'm not, "I've been better, but I've got some nice food later" again, I accept how I'm feeling but hopefully I have a positive to end on. It's a daily conscious decision, I have to work on it and it can be draining, but it's so worth it!

I'm planning on exploring even more, the knee is feeling a lot better now. I'd like to find some ancient ruins, caves and huge forests!

Walking facts worth knowing:

- Just 20-30 minutes a day can improve cardiovascular health and boost energy levels.
- Walking can reduce fatigue in cancer survivors by up to 40% according to some studies.
- Regular walking is linked to lower recurrence rates in certain cancers.
- Spending time in nature is proven to lower blood pressure and stress hormones.
- The steady pace of walking encourages mindfulness, which can improve emotional resilience.

Dressed to De-Stress: Dopamine Dressing

This has honestly been life changing. Maybe I've been doing it longer than I realised, but only recently did I discover it had an actual name: *dopamine dressing*. Clothes as medicine. Clothes as armour. Clothes as a way of saying, "This is me and today I get to decide how I feel."

For me, clothing has never just been fabric. It's personality stitched into cotton, confidence zipped up in a jacket, resilience buttoned down in denim. It can make you feel sharper, braver, even a little bit untouchable.

Sometimes it's not about the obvious stuff; It can be subtle - silly socks, the smell of your favourite aftershave, or a vintage Casio calculator watch that makes you grin every time you check it. These little details are like Easter eggs for the soul, private nods to yourself that say you're still here.

It's funny looking back at my appointments as I would be dressed in the most undignified clothing you can imagine; paper pants with a hole cut out for a camera. They were 'one-size-fits-nobody', crinkly, awkward and a little silly; I guess I really do find humour in the most desperate moments. There's no personality in paper pants, there's no swagger, no confidence, no "me". Hospitals deal in function, not fashion. The gowns are worn over and over, washed at 10,000 degrees (not quite) and faded, their stories gone. Everyone waiting for surgery looked the same, had the same garments that would be quickly removed and thrown into a basket ready to be washed and then put on for the next operation. This was exactly why later on dressing well mattered so much. It wasn't just clothes; It was reclaiming myself.

After my surgery, I couldn't wear anything without an elasticated waist. The scar sat just below my belt line - scabby, sore and tight. Pulling on a pair of jeans felt like punishment and for weeks I lived in joggers and loose T-shirts.

It hit me hard how much clothing had always been a part of my personality. My quirks weren't just inside me - they were visible, stitched into what I wore. Without that outlet, I felt like a duller version of myself.

Initially, I physically struggled to wear the things I loved; My jeans mocked me from the wardrobe, shirts felt tight across my chest and even bending to tie my trainers was impossible. There was this strange gap between who I knew myself to be and who I looked like on the outside. It felt like I'd been dressed in someone else's life. That's why, when I could finally wear those things again, it wasn't just clothing, it was recovery made visible.

I made it a huge part of my recovery routine: get up, eat breakfast, shower, get dressed. But not just *dressed*. No more joggers-and-slobs. Instead, I'd go all in with shirt, trousers, shoes, aftershave. Even if I had no plans to leave the house, it made me feel like life itself was an event, like I mattered. And here's the thing: it worked. It was a small victory against the gloom. My scar might have dictated what I could wear, but my spirit decided *how* I wore it.

Clothing didn't just change how I looked; it changed how I acted. A good outfit shifts your mindset; Put me in joggers and an old T-shirt and I'll slouch, drag my feet, keep my head down. Put me in a Hawaiian shirt and Docs and suddenly my shoulders are back, my head's high and I walk into life like it's a catwalk. You start to feel like the version of yourself you want to be and that spills over into everything else. One outfit can genuinely change the course of a day.

There were still days that I didn't want to get out of bed; Days where the weight of everything pressed down so hard. On one of those mornings, I remember really forcing myself into the shower, spraying on my aftershave and putting on my leopard print shirt. I fancied some chocolate, some snacks and some treats - after all, I deserved them! So, off to the shops I went.

Going to the supermarket dressed up, I first thought, "everyone's going to stare." But no one cared. And even if they did, so what? People's negative opinions are just projections of their own limits, why should I shrink myself to make them comfortable?

The science-y part: dopamine is the brain's reward chemical. It's the spark you feel when you eat your favourite food, hear a song that takes you back to good times, or finally do the washing up that you've avoided for the last few days. It's also what gives that little rush when you put on something that makes you feel good. And "feeling good" doesn't always mean glamour. Sometimes dopamine dressing is your best suit; sometimes it's a hoodie, sometimes it's that fluffy dressing gown - It's about association, about memory, about what lifts you *today*.

There's another layer to this. When you've been through cancer, your body changes. It fluctuates. You gain weight, lose weight, scar, heal, swell, bruise. You don't always recognise yourself in the mirror and in those moments, a single compliment can hit like an electric bolt, supercharging you. That happened to me when I started posting "outfit of the day" videos on TikTok. I expected silence at best, ridicule at worst but what I got instead was support. Real, kind words. "love the jacket", "that shirt is fire", "keep going mate, you're smashing it." It may sound small, but when you're rebuilding yourself, those words land heavy; They tell you you're not invisible, that you can still turn heads. That you still *exist*.

At some point, I decided to add another subtle touch to my outfits: a black onyx necklace. Years earlier I'd treated myself to a thin silver curb chain with an old Italian coin on it. I've always wanted to visit Italy (still on my list!) so it became a kind of talisman, a reminder that life is about places still to see, adventures still to come. But after surgery, I wanted something more. Something that didn't just point to the future, but that gave me strength in the present.

Working in jewellery for over ten years, I'd picked up plenty of knowledge about gemstones and crystals. I wouldn't call myself spiritual, but I do believe in energy. And I believe in science - science saved my life after all. Still, there are things science can't fully explain.

Black onyx is traditionally seen as a protective stone. It's said to absorb negative energy, to ground you when life feels shaky, to give you strength in times of stress. Did I believe it had magical powers? Not really. But here's my take: does it even matter? The placebo effect is real, it's been studied for decades and if holding onto a stone makes me calmer, if it grounds me in the middle of chaos, then that's the only proof I need.

So, I wore it and whenever I felt anxious, I'd catch myself holding the onyx in my hand. I held it before hospital appointments, I held it when I felt nervous about seeing people after surgery, I held it when my mind was racing at 3am. It became my safety net, a physical anchor when my head wanted to spiral off somewhere darker.

It's not about whether black onyx actually absorbs negative energy, what mattered was that it helped me shift my mindset; It gave me something to focus on, a reminder that I wasn't powerless. Just like dopamine dressing, it became another layer of my armour. My clothes gave me confidence, but this little stone gave me grounding and when you're trying to rebuild yourself, you need both.

I need visual stimulation and fashion helps with this. I have other bits of jewellery that I wear every day - a silver horseshoe ring I've had for about 20 years, a tiger's eye ring and a lapis lazuli bracelet that my Mom bought me for one birthday. When you've stared down cancer, you learn the value of defiance. Dressing up became an act of rebellion; It was me saying, "you don't get to flatten me." Every outfit was a middle finger to fear, to doubt, to that creeping thought that life had shrunk.

Sometimes the clothing was loud - floral print shirt, shiny boots, a moustache I let grow wild just because it made me laugh in the mirror. Sometimes it was quiet - a necklace under my shirt, socks only I could see. The scale didn't matter, what mattered was the choice.

People might think clothing is superficial, that it's vanity but here's what I learned: when your world feels out of control, choosing what you wear is one of the few things still in your hands.

Recovery isn't just about medicines and milestones, it's about identity, about piecing yourself back together when you feel scattered. And sometimes a smart jacket, a necklace or a pair of nice trainers can hold more than fabric or metal or leather - they can hold *you*.

So yeah, if someone asks me why I'm dressed up just to buy some tea bags, I'll tell them the truth: because life's too short to live in fear and worry about paper pants.

Trauma and Cancer: More Than Just the Physical Battle

Cancer doesn't just change your body; it changes your entire perception of life. It gets into your head in ways you can't explain to anyone who hasn't been there. The diagnosis alone can hit like an emotional sledgehammer, but the real shock often comes later, when the dust settles and you realise you've been changed in ways you never imagined possible. You're no longer the person you were five minutes ago, that version of you is gone forever and you grieve them - no one warns you about that part.

Trauma in cancer isn't just the big moments or events; it's the endless waiting for test results. It's staying awake until 3am convinced something feels different. It's looking in the mirror and not quite recognising yourself. Even when the treatment ends, your brain doesn't quite understand. You stay hyper-aware of every twinge, every ache, every pain.

It's a series of blows: the appointments, the waiting rooms, the treatments that make you feel worse before they make you better, the uncertainty that follows you like a shadow. Trauma in this context is complex - it's both sudden and slow-burning.

Then there's the reaction from other people. Some friends disappear; It's not always because they don't care – sometimes they just can't handle it – but it still hurts. Others suddenly reappear after fifteen years with a message that starts with, "If there's anything I can do…" And there are the people who carry on like nothing's happening, which can be a relief or completely infuriating depending on the day.

One of the hardest lessons is learning to focus on yourself for the first time in your life. Not in a selfish way, but because you have to. You start to notice who drains your energy and who actually helps you heal. Cutting out toxic people becomes an act of self-preservation. *You* are the priority now.

Cancer shifts your priorities in ways you don't see coming; The petty things fall away and you stop giving time to people or situations that don't matter. You become aware that life isn't endless and that how you spend your days – and who you spend them with – is everything.

This is where trauma and cancer intersect:

- **Hypervigilance**: You notice every new ache or symptom and your mind races to worst-case scenarios.
- **Loss of trust in your body**: The same body that once carried you without fuss has, in your eyes, betrayed you and you wonder why.
- **Shifts in identity**: You are no longer just "you." You are "you, who's had cancer." It changes how others see you and how you see yourself.
- **A reordering of priorities**: Things that once seemed urgent suddenly feel irrelevant and vice versa.

It's important to note that these reactions aren't weakness - they're your mind's way of adapting to what has happened. Psychologists sometimes call this *post-traumatic growth* when it leads to new meaning or resilience, but the road there can be messy and unpredictable.

For many survivors, the trauma doesn't end when the treatment does. The medical world may close your file, but you're left carrying the weight - the knowledge that it could happen again and that life is more fragile than you ever wanted to admit. A surgeon's role is to remove the cancer; they did that and now it's your turn to carry on with life. That knowledge can be heavy, but it can also make you deliberate about how you live. And maybe that's the hardest truth of all: you will never be the same and that's both the loss and the gift.

Birds, birds, birds!

Unfortunately, this isn't the raunchy part of the book (plus my Mom will read this!). Nope, this is actually to do with the birds that visit my garden on a daily basis.

For my Birthday this year, My Mom bought me a bird feeder with a camera attached, after Millsy suggested I'd like it. Set up was easy, the camera was clear and looked amazing, it had its own little perch for the birds to land on that you could fill it up with seeds. I thought it would just be a bit of fun. Something to pass the time, maybe give me a few nice photos and videos to look at. What I didn't expect was how much joy those little visitors would bring me.

There's something magical about seeing a tiny Robin or Blue-tit hop onto the perch, tilting its head as if it knows it's being watched. The footage captures every detail - the way a Jay's bright blue feathers catch the light, the quick flick of a Sparrows tail, the absolute focus as they pick up a sunflower seed.

It's easy to underestimate the value of small, everyday pleasures when you're going through recovery. So much of your life is suddenly about the big things - test results, appointments, the next scan, but birds don't care about any of that. They turn up, they feed and they flutter off again. Watching them is a reminder that life carries on in the simplest, purest ways.

For me, this little hobby has become more than just entertainment; It's a reason to look outside, even on my darkest days. It gets me learning what each visitor is, that a males looks different to a females and that juveniles look different still!

There's plenty of research showing that spending time with nature improves mental wellbeing and garden birds are one of the easiest ways to bring nature to you. Watching them lowers stress levels, encourages mindfulness and can even help ease feelings of isolation. You don't have to go far - they come to you!

Feeding birds is a two-way act; You give them food and a safe perch, they give you beauty, movement and company. It's a quiet exchange, but it's enough to lift your mood, especially on days when you're feeling low. And the camera? That just makes it even better. You can replay their visits, share them with friends, or simply watch again on the days when you need cheering up.

The best part is that you never quite know who will turn up next. One day it's the regulars - the Great-tit, the Robins or House Sparrows and another day it's a surprise guest, a bird you've never seen before and may never see again! Each visit feels like a small gift.

My first visitor was a Bluetit, who I named Frank. Why Frank you ask? Well, he looked like a Frank! I was so mesmerised by him, his colours, his movement. I wanted to feed him, look after him! Over the next few weeks, my feeder became more and more active. New bird feed (meal worms and suet pellets) attracted more species and each new arrival brought something different, something amazing. Nature is so incredible!

Woodpeckers: by far my favourites. Sometimes two at once; one clinging to the side, the other perched on top. One day, I saw something that floored me - one woodpecker feeding the other. Beak to beak, gentle and deliberate. I researched it and it's done out of love. I sat there thinking: *How beautiful is that?* And also, *Why can't I find love like that??*

Robins: the sweethearts of the garden. They hop in like tiny guardians, always watching, always calm. Their fledglings have pure attitude, moving for no one!

Blue tits & Great tits: cheeky little gymnasts, darting in and out so fast you barely see them. Great tits in particular remind me of Frank, my first visitor and unofficial "landlord" of the feeder.

Jays: absolute showstoppers. When the camera catches their wings with that electric flash of blue, it feels like fireworks going off in the middle of an ordinary morning. Powerful, bold and unapologetically themselves.

Goldfinches: only ever visited once, but I have my hopes that they will return. Delicate little artists with splashes of yellow like they've been painted by hand.

Blackbirds (and their partners): the males are sleek and serious with a bright yellow beak, whilst the females softer and more understated. Together, they feel like the old married couple of the garden - reliable, calm and always turning up for their dinners.

House sparrows: the noisy neighbours. Always in groups, always bickering, always sticking their beaks in where they don't belong. You can't help but laugh at their curiosity. I counted 14 in my garden at one point, all fluttering up and down and off the feeder!

Nuthatches: Millsy's favourite. They actually weigh the seeds; it has to be right, or they chuck it out! Beautiful looking.

Starlings: a lot bigger than I imagined! The juvenile has incredible bellies, bright blue with small white spots!

Magpies: dramatic, clever, and not afraid to throw their weight around. Not exactly my favourite visitor.

Fledglings: my favourite surprise visitors. Scruffy, unsure, feathers not quite ready, but full of possibility. There's something hilarious about watching them, looking confused, trying to learn about the world around them.

Pigeons: oh, you buggers! Deffo not my favourite. Greedy and unbothered. Nonchalant. Will eat until ALL the seed is gone and not allow anyone else near.

One thing I didn't expect was how much these feathery visitors would inspire me to draw them. I'd started sketching animals as a way to heal but drawing these real visitors - the ones who actually came to *my* garden - felt different. Frank became one of my first bird sketches, followed by a cheeky Robin. It wasn't just art; it was a connection. I was honouring the little visitors that had cheered me up when I needed it most.

Now onto Squirrels…my fluffy nemesis. Oh, you little blighters!! I used to love squirrels, but we have now had a major fallout. Squirrels are cool, they're cheeky, mischievous, cute, funny and on the whole harmless. Well, that was my view before the bird feeder!

I haven't had a squirrel in my garden the whole time I've lived here, 6 and a half years, or at least none that I've never noticed. Day by day, a squirrel would scurry up the pole onto the bird feeder and stay there and eat - for hours on end. Three weeks' worth of bird feed, gone, just like that. They must've thought it was an all you can eat buffet. They're acrobatic, fast, and wily. I had to do my research to outwit them. Let's try peppermint oil - didn't work. Let's try mirrors, not bothered. Shouting at them - not fussed one iota! I really didn't want to do something too drastic in case it scared off the birds.

One day, the squirrel kissed the camera, I kid you not! The utter defiance!! That was the final straw, how dare you! Finally, I found something that may work, a "Baffle". A small plastic dome, you put below the feeder; basically, the squirrel would climb the pole, then look up and be "baffled" as they were unable to go any further, the shape of the dome meant they were unable to climb above or around it. Have that! For some reason, I felt slightly guilty. Afterall, they were only trying their best to survive and have a nice bit of food. So, I bought a little wooden Squirrel house, just for them, the other end of the garden.

In a strange way, the birds have taught me patience. You can't rush them; you can't predict them. You just have to wait, watch and be ready to enjoy the moment when it happens. And that's a good lesson for life after cancer - to slow down, to notice, to be present for the small things that make life richer.

Feeding Yourself Back to Strength

One thing I learned early on is that food isn't just fuel - it's part of recovery. After cancer treatment your body is working overtime to heal, rebuild and find its balance again. What you eat can make that process easier, calmer and even more enjoyable.

I focus on food every single day, and I see that as a positive. Planning meals, thinking about flavours and textures, even just imagining what I'm going to cook - it's one of the highlights of my day. Food gives me something to look forward to, something that feels creative and nourishing all at once.

Being vegetarian, I've had so many people ask whether I get "enough" protein or if I feel restricted without eating meat. The truth is, I don't see it that way. If anything, recovery has made me more conscious of what I'm putting into my body, not less. I think of every meal as an opportunity to give my body what it needs - not just to survive but to thrive.

After cancer it's not just about calories. It's about nourishment; Vegetables, fruits, whole grains, nuts, seeds and pulses are full of vitamins, minerals and antioxidants that help the body repair. I've found that eating a wide variety of plant-based foods isn't just healthy, it's colourful, fresh and far from boring. I've tried SO many different foods from being a vegetarian, way more than I did when I simply ate chicken, rice and broccoli most days. Finding new flavours and styles is so invigorating.

Fruit is a huge part of my diet. I love having chopped fruit with Greek yoghurt, mixing in goji berries, seeds, nuts and a sprinkle of bee pollen. It's a bowl full of goodness that tastes like a treat and leaves me feeling energised rather than weighed down. For me, food has to be both satisfying and supportive - I want to enjoy every bite.

Protein is important for healing and I find mine in lentils, chickpeas, tofu, quinoa, broccoli and more! Add some spices and here we go to flavour town!

It's easy to overlook hydration too but drinking enough water helps with fatigue, supports digestion and keeps your body running smoothly. It's such a simple thing but I've noticed that on days when I forget to drink enough, I feel it - sluggish, headachy and just not myself. I prob drink about 10-15 cups of tea every day and a brew really does solve a lot!

Nutrition during recovery isn't about strict rules or denying yourself the things you enjoy. I don't exclude treats; Ice cream, dark chocolate, some monster munch, a nice glass of red wine - they all have their place. I just try to keep them in balance. I see them as something I've earned after going through such a serious and intrusive operation, but I also know that I need to look after myself in the long run. It's not about guilt, it's about care.

Cooking has become a kind of therapy for me. One of my favourite rituals is making a pizza from scratch. Measuring the flour, kneading the dough, covering it to prove, then folding it every few hours - the process is slow, calm and natural. I crack on a bit of Dean Martin and sing along while I make my own sauce, then open a nice bottle of red as it cooks. It's not just about the meal at the end; it's about the mindfulness of the process and the feeling of creating something with love.

Eating well doesn't mean you'll never feel tired or low, but it gives you a better foundation to cope when those moments come. It's about giving your body the best chance to do its job of healing. Cancer changes the way you look at food. It's no longer about diets, fads or what's trending on social media, it's about simple, real food that supports you day after day. For me, that's most likely the vegetarian stable of a stir fry, a bean chilly or a vegetable curry. Sometimes, it's a scoop of ice cream eaten in the garden on a sunny afternoon - because joy is part of healing too.

In the end, eating well is another form of self-respect. You're telling your body, "I value you. I want you to heal. I want you to keep going." And that, I think, is one of the most powerful things you can do for yourself during recovery.

Survivor's Guilt

When people talk about cancer survival, they like to frame it in a simple way; You're either fighting it or you've beaten it. In my case I was a "warrior," a miracle, the one who "made it". People clap you on the back, tell you how inspiring you are, then go back to their lives. On the surface, it sounds lovely, who wouldn't want to be the person who "won"? But what people rarely see is the shadow that comes with survival - guilt.

It sneaks up on you. You don't plan it. You don't sit there thinking, *I'm going to ruin my own good news with a dose of misery.* But it's there. Guilt that you made it through when others didn't. Guilt that your operation worked, your recovery is moving along, while someone else with the same cancer never had that chance. Survivor's guilt is a phrase more often associated with soldiers, disasters and accidents. But cancer survivors know it just as well.

For me, it's been hard to shake the thought that I just got "lucky". It's not about being ungrateful, it's not that I don't want to be here - of course I do. It's the quiet voice that whispers: *Why me? Why am I standing here, when someone else isn't?*

You can't help but think about the flip of the coin; If a few things had gone differently - and I know that more than most because of the delay in my diagnosis - I might not be writing this book at all.

There are other shades to this guilt. It's not just about life and death. Sometimes it's about feeling guilty for struggling when you "should" be happy. People assume once you're through surgery, through recovery, that life returns to normal, that you should be skipping down the road, full of joy and constantly looking forward. But the truth is, there's no "normal" to return to. You're changed; Physically, mentally, emotionally - you don't get the old version of you back and yet you can feel guilty for saying that out loud, as if you're ungrateful.

I've caught myself feeling guilty over the smallest of things; Guilty for being tired when I want to sleep all afternoon -shouldn't I be "making the most out of life"? Guilty for snapping at someone because fatigue has taken every ounce of patience I have. I can suffer with mood swings and take it out on the most important person in my life, my Mom. She has the patience of a saint, she supports me so much and for that I am eternally grateful. I can feel guilty for laughing and feeling good one moment, then low and fearful the next. Guilty because I know someone else would give anything to be in my shoes, yet here I am grumbling about needing a nap. It sounds ridiculous when you write it down, but in the moment it's heavy.

Another layer is the expectation. Once you're "a survivor", people want you to be a walking poster for hope. They want to see you running marathons, jumping out of planes for charity, raising money for the cause. They want inspiration, the happy ending, the motivational quotes, and of course, part of me wants to be that too. But when you have a bad day - when the scar aches or your mind wanders to the what ifs - you feel like you're letting people down. The pressure to always be positive can be its own burden. Survivor's guilt feeds on that.

It also creeps in when you start to think about the future. There are moments where I catch myself making plans - holidays, projects, even just a nice dinner - and then I wonder, *Should I be allowed to look forward when others didn't get that chance?* The comparison trap is brutal. Reading about someone who didn't survive, or who had a far harder road than mine, makes me question whether I have the right to complain or even the right to dream. Yet, I can't compare my journey with anyone else's; Comparison is the thief of joy.

Here's the truth: guilt doesn't mean you're ungrateful. Guilt is really a sign of compassion. It means you see the unfairness of the world, you feel the weight of other people's pain and you care enough to carry some of it. That doesn't make you broken. It makes you human.

What I've learnt is that guilt can't be ignored. If you try to shove it away, it only grows. What helps is reframing it; Instead of seeing survival as an undeserved gift, I try to see it as a responsibility. I survived, so what can I do with that survival? Maybe it's as simple as living honestly, enjoying the silly things, laughing, making art, listening to music, cooking with joy. Maybe it's writing this book so someone else doesn't feel alone in their own guilt.

There was a moment not long ago when I was sitting in the garden, cup of tea in hand, watching the bird's squabble over the feeder. I felt peaceful, then out of nowhere that guilt nudged in - *why do you get to have this?* My first instinct was to push it away, but instead I let it sit. I realised that maybe the best way to honour those who didn't make it is to fully live the life I still have. To savour the peace, the silliness, the food, the music. To waste nothing, not even an afternoon watching sparrows.

Survivor's guilt may never fully go away, but it doesn't have to rule you. If anything, it can sharpen your sense of purpose. It can remind you to love harder, laugh louder and cut the toxic nonsense from your life because, frankly, there's no time for it. It can remind you to focus on what matters - your health, your family, your passions, the small daily joys.

If you're feeling this guilt yourself, know this: you're not alone. It's not weakness and it's not wrong. You deserve to be here. You deserve to live, to laugh, to plan, to mess up, to succeed, to have lazy days and brilliant ones. Survival is not about living perfectly. It's about living - fully, messily, honestly.

So yes, I carry survivor's guilt. Some days it feels heavier than others, but I carry it alongside hope, humour, music and love. And that's what keeps me moving forward.

Strength in Number: Cancer as a Community and Support Network

Going through cancer can be isolating and insular. You feel alone, lost, by yourself. Your body has turned on you for no reason whatsoever. You question everything and sometimes there are simply no answers.

At one point I decided I wanted to speak to others, maybe join a group, meet up and share experiences. Unfortunately, there wasn't anything local. The nearest support group was a forty-five-minute drive away and with fatigue as bad as mine that just wasn't possible.

Then I saw there was a Macmillan coffee morning at the local M&S. Perfect! Fifteen minutes away, tunes on in the car, something upbeat (for me that means the 80s). Billy Ocean came on and by the time I pulled into the car park I was in great spirits! I walked in expecting to see tables of people, maybe balloons and signs pointing me to a group of survivors sharing cake and conversation. Instead, nothing. No groups. No signs. I went to the café and asked where the coffee morning was.

"Oh, yeah, it's more of a charity thing, we just donate."

Not quite the supportive gathering I was hoping for. Still, I bought myself a coffee and sat down. Being on my own in those situations always feels awkward. Do I look up and smile at strangers or keep my head down? Do I try to look relaxed or busy? I probably drank my coffee faster than anyone in the history of M&S before wandering through the funky shirt section and heading home. Not what I expected but at least I got out of the house and gave it a go.

What really made a difference for me was talking to other cancer survivors online, listening to what they had been through, what they endured, the way they adapted and coped. Some stories were heartbreaking, some were uplifting, but every single one of them gave me something. The word that stuck out the most from all those conversations was empathy.

The kindness I felt from people I had never met was incredible. The constant messages of "you're doing well" and "keep going" carried me through some of my hardest days. People who had battled breast cancer three times, people managing skin cancer, people living with terminal diagnoses, all telling me how strong I was and that I should believe in myself. If they could still be hopeful, then so could I. That power from a shared experience was something I will never forget.

Support from doctors and nurses is vital but it is professional whereas support from other survivors is something else entirely. There is no need to explain the fear, the exhaustion, the way your mind runs away with "what ifs". They already know. And when someone knows without you needing to say a word, that is real comfort.

I also found humour was part of the connection. Not making light of cancer itself but laughing at the bizarre things you end up talking about. Comparing notes on strange medical terms or sharing stories of an intrusive camera up "there". Laughter doesn't erase the pain, but it makes it easier to carry.

Community is not always easy though. When you open yourself up to the stories of others you also open yourself up to grief. Sometimes you lose people you have connected with. Sometimes you read updates that remind you just how cruel cancer can be. It can be overwhelming, but even then, even in the sadness, there is a sense of being part of something bigger than yourself. You are not carrying it all alone.

Over time I realised community is not just about receiving support, it is also about giving it; Sharing my experiences, encouraging others, even just listening, gave me a sense of purpose. It reminded me that survival is not about going back to how things were, it is about finding new meaning.

Cancer may feel like it isolates you but there is a whole world of people out there who understand. Sometimes you just have to look in unexpected places. For me it wasn't a coffee morning with cake and chatter. It was a group of strangers online who became friends. People who would message me daily, Kelly, Mel, Chrissy, Evelyn.

The biggest lesson I learned is this: connection heals in its own way. It may not remove the pain or the fear, but it makes those feelings easier to bear. Community gives you hope, strength, humour, and belief. And it reminds you that even when cancer tries to isolate you, you are never truly on your own.

Knee Op: Yes, ANOTHER Operation

The idea was simple, I was off work, recovering. My only form of exercise and getting fresh air was my walks. My knee started to play up again; Pains and aches after walking an hour. A cyst would form on the outside of the knee, large and incredibly painful (and my mind immediately goes to cancer). My walks would now be 30 minutes instead of an hour, I'd hobble back, in pain and I'd feel that pain for 2-3 days. The walks went down to 15 minutes and I'd struggle. Something needed doing.

I'd already had a knee op two years previously. That was the first time I was put under anaesthetic for an op, surely now I was an expert in that field! The injuries had stemmed from playing football. Now, I wasn't exactly Juan Pablo Angel, but it was fantastic exercise and a great way to see the lads and have some banter. The injury? Not so great. Instead of my ankle breaking, the knee took the brunt and that turned out to be worse; Career ending as it were. I never risked playing football again, it was a choice that made sense, I didn't want to be in pain, to limp around, to get more injuries. This was serious enough!

I do have one everlasting memory from my time playing Power league in Aston; the best goal ever scored...well, the best one I've ever scored! Deano spotted me wide on the wing, he pinged a beautiful ball, 30 yards, I tracked it, watched the flight perfectly and then BANG! A volley ala Steve McManaman in his Real Madrid days, the most perfect volley I've ever hit in my life. The connection felt incredible, and it soared into the top corner. At least, that's how I remember it!

I got back in touch with the medical team and surgeon, a fantastic guy, very personable and friendly. We talked, I discussed the pain and why I wanted it sorted. Yes, I played the cancer card - you have to! Don't wanna go anywhere? "Well, I have had cancer" don't wanna be ripped off? "Anything you can do would be amazing, I mean, I have just had cancer". Don't wanna wait for appointments, you guessed it, crack out the fact you've had cancer. It's also a light-hearted almost sarcastic way with dealing with that pain and trauma; you're using it and taking the power back.

After some scans on the knee, it was suggested that keyhole surgery would be needed. The knee showed two tears, the meniscus and my anterior cruciate ligament (ACL). My thought process was that I may as well have the knee operation. What's the point in waiting? I'm home, so when I get back to work, I didn't want to suddenly go, "oh yeah, I need time off for an op"!

I didn't have to wait long for the appointment but things didn't exactly go as simple as I'd hoped. The operation went well, keyhole again. However, I woke up and had to have a brace fitted, something that I'd have to wear for 6 weeks, 24/7 apart from taking it off for a max of one hour a day to clean myself and let my leg breathe a little. I honestly didn't know this was part of the recovery, I have no recollection of this being told to me previous to the operation.

The brace turned into something I despised. Hard to sleep, hard to move around, itchy, sweaty, smelly. I hated every single moment in it. It had a 90° rotation, which would allow my knee to bend, but I'd need to use crutches for two weeks. My Mom offered to live with me again. Yet again, there was no way I could've coped without her, have you ever tried to carry a cuppa and use two crutches? Impossible!

The pain was there still; any slight twist or turn was a huge no no. I'd also have to have A LOT of physiotherapy for it. Turns out this knee op was a pretty serious one.

I eventually got out the house, using the crutches, very slowly and carefully down the steps to the pavement, my Mom watching on anxiously: "I'll be back in 15 mins".

I was determined to get to the end of the road and back. You have to give yourself a goal, a challenge, one that's achievable but that pushes you. Then, you can push yourself further each time or aim too at least. It's not all about smashing your targets, it's about attempting to.

Each day I'd do a little bit more, if I could but some days, I simply needed more rest. Before long, the two crutches went down to one. I found it easier to get up and down my stairs that way. Two weeks passed and it was now time to stop using them. I think I walked around a little like Robocop the first few days, slowly, but surely getting to my target - the kettle! I think by now you know I love my tea!

My mom moved back to hers but wasn't far if I needed help. She'd come every few days to make sure I was OK. Millsy would be back on our Tuesday night FIFA sessions. Do I regret having it? I'm still unsure and I think the timing was bad. I should've waited until my cancer recovery was further along; I really struggled mentally in those first 6 week, that brace set me back so much, I was so angry and upset. But it's done.

8 months of physio every 3-6 weeks. The advice was to use it. My hamstrings are weak, build them back up, get

back to the gym. Good ol' Gaz got me a gym pass. Hold on, was life getting some normality back at last?

Recovery was slow, painful and hard. I had to really push myself, strain on the leg presses, stretch and be super careful; not too much too soon. I knew I needed an operation if I was to continue my walks; Walking gives me way more than just exercise, it offers me peace, a place to get away from the noise, a place to connect with nature and to forget about life. This was the reason I chose to have the knee op, so I can't regret that decision.

Discovering My Identity

I'd changed. But into who, into what? Cancer does that to you. It strips you down to the bare bones of yourself and forces you to rebuild. I could be whoever I wanted to be, but who was that?

I've developed nuances that have come out of nowhere; I get overwhelmed extremely easily and that's new to me. Before cancer, I was the person who could simultaneously take in a room, a conversation, background noise and multitask successfully - that was part and parcel of my role as a Producer. Now, too many voices, too many tasks, or even just a wall of information can feel like the world closing in on me. I never used to understand what people meant when they said they were "overstimulated," but now I get it. My brain sometimes just throws up its hands and says, "enough." I can struggle with even a simple decision - what to eat, what to do first, where to start this book - it can all feel like too much. Maybe it's the sheer volume of information I've had to process over the last year and a half; Hospitals, treatments, risks, statistics, percentages, side effects - my brain has been on high alert for so long that it's like it's hit capacity. Some days it feels like there's no more room for anything else. But here's the thing: noticing that overwhelming feeling has forced me to slow down, to strip things back, to simplify and reassess.

I've found ways to ground myself; Instead of having the TV on as background noise I prefer to simply sit quietly with a cuppa, if I get anxious or start to get a headache, I reach for my black onyx necklace. Little physical anchors that remind me I'm here, I'm safe and I don't have to respond to everything at once. To slow down and just breathe.

Depression had beaten me down over the years. It had destroyed my worth and value. I'd spend hours making up scenarios that weren't real. Sometimes this would affect me for weeks, I'd play them over and over again, usually at the quiet of night, affecting my sleep, causing me headaches. Sometimes something random from my past would pop into my head, maybe something I wasn't happy with and I'd relive it, think about the what ifs, "maybe I should've said this or said that", "what if THEY said this or did that?" It was a vicious cycle with no winners and one person who definitely lost the fights and the arguments...me. I'd hyper fixate and focus on the minute details; I find it hard to switch off when I have something on my mind, I feel like need to resolve it, but rarely can, so it's a vicious cycle and feels like some sort of self-punishment.

I always think of my thoughts as a tree with branches. Those thought branches veer off in so many different directions, creating more and more branches, twigs, leaves etc. The cycle continues and sometimes I have to work backwards, trying to find where the thought process started and why I'm suddenly thinking about the fact that animals who lay eggs don't have belly buttons. FACT!

Through therapy, I'm honestly able to calm this down more and even stop it dead in its tracks. So, what did I want out of life? I knew one thing for sure - nothing is given to you. You have to fight for it, work for it, sweat for it. Even in the middle of the hardest thing I'd ever faced, that truth hadn't changed. If anything, it felt louder. I'd come through something that had tried to take me out, and yet here I was. Still standing, still thinking, still wondering. The question wasn't "why me?" anymore. It was "who do I want to be now?"

It's funny how something as small as facial hair can spark a revelation. I'll never forget the first time I grew a moustache. It was years before cancer, for Movember. At the time, it was a bit of fun, a daft excuse to look like a 70s detective for a month all in the name of charity. But you know what? I loved it. Properly loved it. The moustache suited me in a way I hadn't expected. The problem? December 1st arrived and with it the unwritten law of Movember: you shave it off. I did so, reluctantly, at midnight. My girlfriend at the time had never seen me clean-shaven until that moment. Maybe that was the beginning of the end of our relationship (kidding…sort of).

Fast forward to after my treatment and something in me clicked. One day I decided to trim my beard down and leave the moustache a little longer. It made me smile. A few days later, I trimmed it more. Before I knew it, the moustache had taken centre stage and it made me laugh every time I caught sight of myself in the mirror. Then I thought, sod it. Let's wet shave the lot and keep the 'tache. And you know what? I looked amazing! Honestly, I was chuffed with myself. Proper Tom Selleck vibes, minus the Miami tan and palm trees - I definitely had the shirts though! It wasn't serious, it wasn't planned, but it was *mine*. Rockstars were doing it, actors were doing it, so why couldn't I? Who says moustaches are only for hipsters in coffee shops? There's this weird unspoken rule in society that unless you're famous you "can't" dress like that or grow that style, or look that way. Well, who the hell made that rule? I say break it. Embrace it. See the funny side. Grow a moustache and love it.

I realised, post-cancer, that I was done with that nonsense. Life was too fragile, too unpredictable, to live by rules written by people I didn't even know. So, I grew the moustache and I loved it. Loved the daftness, loved the rebellion, loved that it made me laugh. It wasn't just hair on my face - it was a reminder that I was still here, still capable of choosing who I wanted to be.

The truth is that identity isn't about impressing anyone else. It's about how you see yourself when no one's looking. Did I still feel attractive? Did I still feel like me? The moustache said yes. Maybe I was still single, but who cares? If you can look in the mirror and smile, that's a victory.

The moustache was just the start. I wasn't going full goth or reinventing myself completely, but I was experimenting. Cancer had taken so much control from me, but here was an area where I had complete say. No consultant could tell me what to wear, no surgeon could dictate my hair or my clothes. This was mine. I remember putting on an old leather jacket and catching myself in the reflection. I stood taller (all 5'5" of me), I looked sharper, I felt stronger. You don't always have to feel strong on the inside straight away, sometimes it starts with how you look on the outside. Put the jacket on, wear the boots and suddenly you're standing straighter. That little bit of armour gets you through the day.

Music became another lifeline. I started making playlists that felt like identity markers. Some days it was heavy rock blasting through my headphones, drowning out the fear with noise and power, other days it was something atmospheric and sometimes even daft pop songs when I needed a laugh. There was one night I made a cup of tea and danced round the kitchen to "I'm Still Standing" by Elton John. Ridiculous, yes. But also, exactly what I needed. And isn't that what identity is? A patchwork of all the things that make you feel alive.

Of course, other people noticed these little changes. Some mates laughed at the moustache, some loved it. My Mom wasn't sure at first but said it "suited me"; That's Mom-code for "I don't quite get it, but I'll support you." And that was the point. People will always have their opinions, but your identity isn't a committee decision. It's yours.

I thought about labels a lot. Patient. Survivor. Victim. None of them felt quite right. Yes, I was a cancer patient, yes, I'd had to survive more than I thought I could, but I didn't want those words to be my whole story. I was also a son, a mate, a bloke with a moustache who liked horror films and pizza and a biker jackets. A human being, not just a diagnosis. There's power in reminding yourself of that. You're not just what has happened to you, you're what you choose to do next.

Talking of labels, something my identity had was tattoos. I knew I wanted to have something to represent what I'd just been through, yes, I had the scar, but I wanted another permanent reminder of my endurance, my courage, my fight. I had no choice over the scar, how it would look, what shape it would take over time, if it fades etc but, I had a choice in what tattoo I could get; Something permanent to remind me of what I'd been through and how far I'd come.

I knew I wanted a word, below my neck, sort of on the shirt line so that it could be covered up if I had to button up a shirt for whatever reason. But what word? What word would symbolise everything I'd been through? I went through various options but nothing felt right. Then my Mom said "warrior". The amount of people that called me a warrior online, this was it; the synergy I felt from this word was empowering.

I contacted Ally and booked in a day session. I hadn't been in a year, but everyone recognised me! I love that tattoo shop and as soon as I walked in, Ally made me a brew! We discussed the tattoo, placement, font etc and then the transfer was on, it was time, lie back and let it happen. It didn't hurt as much as I'd remembered the others did, I mean, it still hurt, but maybe because it meant so much, my mind went elsewhere. She was very gentle and knew how significant this was for me.

I also decided I may as well have a few others whilst I was there, some Viking runes on my hands, left hand "courage", right hand "strength". It felt so good to have these etched onto me.

Identity after cancer isn't about finding one final version of yourself and sticking to it forever, it's about realising you can keep changing. You can try new looks, new music, new ways of living. You can laugh at yourself in the mirror; you can find strength in boots or moustaches or tattoos. You can decide every single day who you want to be. For me, that realisation was huge. It gave me hope. It gave me joy. It gave me something solid to stand on in a world that had felt shaky for too long.

It's never too late to find yourself, to learn, to grow, to change. I've adapted to my new life, my new way of thinking. I'm kinder, more humble and have more empathy. Be who you want to be, life is too short to be anything else.

Top Tips

Acceptance: accept the diagnosis, it's not going anywhere. The sooner you do this, the sooner you can move on.

Ask for help: people WILL be there for you.

Talk it through: I wasn't embarrassed to discuss my condition with close friends and family, which helped me feel less alone. Stay close to the people that build you up, not tear you down.

Be prepared: Knowing what to expect made a huge difference. I researched, asked questions, and made sure I understood the procedures and why they mattered.

Be kind to yourself!! You're going through the biggest thing in your life.

Don't RUSH! It's your recovery, not someone else's. Listen to your body. I couldn't bend down to tie my shoelaces for 6 months and only started stretching my stomach after 8/9 months. Take your time.

Find distractions: Drawing, walking in nature, and connecting with my support network helped keep my mind off things.

Mental health support: Dealing with a cancer and/or a chronic condition can take its toll, so getting help through therapy was vital for me.

This Isn't the End, This Is Just the Beginning

When I look back at everything that's happened, it's hard to believe that it all fits into one lifetime, let alone the last year and a half. There were moments that I thought I'd reached the very edge of myself, days where I was convinced that I had nothing left to give. Nights where the weight of it all pressed down so heavily that I could hardly breathe. But here I am. And here you are. You are stronger than you think, braver than you feel and more loved than you realise.

I've learned that cancer doesn't just test your body - it tests your patience, your self-belief, your sense of humour and sometimes your ability to remember where you put the tea bags. It pushes you to the edge, then quietly invites you to build a new edge somewhere else, one you didn't know you could reach.

There's a lot I can't control - and believe me, I've tried. But what I *can* control is how I choose to live with what's happened. I can choose to fill my days with things that matter, with walks that feel like small adventures, with drawing, cooking, feeding the garden birds, laughing at daft things, wearing clothes that make me feel alive. I can choose to take care of myself not out of fear, but out of love. I choose who I want to spend my time with, it's invaluable.

The journey in this book wasn't about "getting back to normal" - I don't think there ever was a normal - it's about building a new kind of life. Learning from each part of adversity I faced, learning who I am and who I want to be. So, learn to enjoy the small moments; the way the sun hits your face, the birds chirping, the way people that love you look at you. Learn that life isn't perfect, it doesn't have to be and that's what makes it so exciting.

Ironically cancer has been the best thing that's happened in my life. It's changed me. For the better. I've discovered things about myself that I would never have known or unlocked. I learned to be proud of myself, acknowledge myself, celebrate the wins and focus my energy.

I still get the odd twinge and ache, scar tissue left over from two major surgeries, a subtle reminder now and then of what I've been through. The various scars can sometimes itch and feel tight. I moisturised them daily for about 6 months to help. The scar is a huge part of who I am. I was looking through my phone's camera roll the other day, seeing pictures of my appendix operation and something didn't look right…oh yeah, no scar down my stomach! It looked odd, almost like I didn't recognise the person I was before.

The fear of cancer never goes away. It's hiding there, a worry that I'll always live with. However, I get regular check-ups, blood tests, appointments, CT scans. Every year I'll need a complex colonoscopy to remove any polyps due to my SPS. Last week I started to feel under the weather, a normal head cold, stuffy nose and sore eyes. Going through something as serious as cancer, I actually forgot that I could just get a cold or a blocked nose and it wouldn't fill me with fear or dread. I could still be ill in other ways and that was weirdly liberating. For once, I didn't dread man flu!

Engaging with therapy was one of the best decisions of my life. I needed help and it's changed me forever. I learnt balance and acceptance. I learnt I could fail and it's actually ok.

The biggest lesson I've learnt throughout all of this? I finally love myself, who I am, who I've become, what I've endured and overcome. I LOVE myself. Writing that is huge. Saying that is HUGE.

Finally, to you, reading this - whether you're facing your own storm or just looking for a bit of hope - I want you to know that life is still out there waiting for you. Not the life you had before maybe, but something new, something surprising, something worth stepping towards.

This isn't the end.

It's not an ending at all.

This is just the beginning.

Special Thanks

Mom, Millsy, Big Man, Deano, Gaz, Clarkey, Mark, Jay, Kelly, Mel, Chrissy, Evelyn, Layla, Mimi, Di, My TikTok friends, Kee Kee, Guy, Hannah, John, Irish Matt, Mr Shariff and his team, Mr Dattani, EPOC, Prof Beggs, MacMillan

Printed in Dunstable, United Kingdom

67872707R00109